# Sustaining Democracy

# Sustaining Democracy

*What We Owe to the Other Side*

ROBERT B. TALISSE

OXFORD
UNIVERSITY PRESS

# OXFORD
UNIVERSITY PRESS

Oxford University Press is a department of the University of Oxford. It furthers
the University's objective of excellence in research, scholarship, and education
by publishing worldwide. Oxford is a registered trade mark of Oxford University
Press in the UK and certain other countries.

Published in the United States of America by Oxford University Press
198 Madison Avenue, New York, NY 10016, United States of America.

Library of Congress Cataloging-in-Publication Data
Names: Talisse, Robert B., author.
Title: Sustaining democracy : what we owe to the other side / Robert B. Talisse.
Description: New York, NY, United States of America :
Oxford University Press, [2021] | Includes bibliographical references and index.
Identifiers: LCCN 2021015057 | ISBN 9780197556450 (hardback) |
ISBN 9780197556474 (epub)
Subjects: LCSH: Democracy. | Citizenship. | Political participation. |
Opposition (Political science) | Equality. | Polarization (Social sciences)—
Political aspects.
Classification: LCC JC423 .T2753 2021 |
DDC 323.6/5—dc23
LC record available at https://lccn.loc.gov/2021015057

DOI: 10.1093/oso/9780197556450.001.0001

1 3 5 7 9 8 6 4 2

Printed by Sheridan Books, Inc., United States of America

# Contents

# Preface

Writing a book is never easy. In the case of this particular book, the usual challenges were magnified by two special circumstances: the 2020 US presidential election and the COVID-19 pandemic. As for the latter, this book was written under lockdown from a small desk in a corner of my home between April and November 2020. Hence the process was stranger than usual. I typically work in my campus office, where I can count on there being long stretches of solitude that every so often are broken by colleagues who see fit to check in on me. A lot of good can result from unexpected chitchat with a philosopher. Even small talk can refresh one's philosophical perspective. Anyway, this book was written outside of the normal course of such exchanges with my regular cast of academic interlocutors. I don't believe the book is *worse* for that, but it was harder to write. That my final chapter makes the argument that democratic citizens need to establish a kind of political distance that can occasionally disconnect them from the din of partisanship is an irony that's not lost on me.

When I began the project, I realized that I would be writing during the ramp-up to the 2020 presidential election. I expected that the period leading up to Election Day would be taxing. My central concern was to insulate the book from anything that would render it *too* topical, too connected to the travails of 2020. However, that the pandemic *itself* became a campaign issue added to the toll of the election season. The resulting circumstances were not ideal for writing a book about the possibility that democracy could be self-defeating—that, even at its best, democracy is exposed to internal dysfunctions that can undermine it. After all, the combination of the election and the pandemic made manifest many of these dysfunctions. At several points along the way, the idea of writing a philosophy book about democracy seemed slightly perverse— a kind of fiddling amid the torching of Rome. Life's too short to bother with anything that makes it feel longer. And yet here we are.

I would not call this an optimist book. But it is a hopeful one. It confronts a serious problem for democracy and then discerns a way in which that problem could be mitigated. This book derives hope from the possibility of citizens reorienting their relationships with their own political commitments—not by withdrawing from them, but instead by understanding them in light of the realization of our vulnerability to certain social and cognitive forces. To me, the cover image conveys this message perfectly. It is a painting by Ian Thuillier titled "Democracy Is DEAD." As I see it, the painting depicts a kind of psychological hazard that is part of the profile of democratic citizenship, a dynamic that gets inside our heads and draws us to the thought that democracy is dying, if not already dead. In this sense, the image is a kind of self-portrait of the democratic citizen, a depiction of our partisan selves. It may sound paradoxical, but the message of this book is that political hope depends on our ability to recognize democracy's vulnerabilities in a way that does not fix on our opposition's flaws, but instead turns inward and recognizes our own political weaknesses.

# Acknowledgments

Although this book was written under conditions of social distancing, I incurred many debts in writing it. I thank the following friends and colleagues for reading chapters, offering advice, and providing encouragement: Kristoffer Ahlstrom-Vij, Scott Aikin, Theano Apostolou, Donna Baker, Elizabeth Barnes, Joe Biehl, William J. Booth, Oliver Burkeman, Ann Cacoullos, Steven Cahn, Michael Calamari, Gregg Caruso, Myisha Cherry, Martin Cohen, Matthew Cotter, John Danaher, Boudewijn de Bruin, Jeroen de Ridder, Catarina Dutilh Novaes, Elizabeth Edenberg, Carrie Figdor, Elizabeth Fiss, Georgi Gardiner, Sandy Goldberg, Dwight Goodyear, Michael Hannon, Nicole Hassoun, Nicole Heller, Diana Heney, D. Micah Hester, David Hildebrand, Julie Hwang, Tziporah Kasachkoff, David Kaspar, Dan Kaufman, John Lachs, Lauren Leydon-Hardy, Katherine Loevy, Michael Lynch, Lisa Madura, Mason Marshall, Chris C. Martin, Takunda Matose, Dave McCullough, Amy McKiernan, Josh Miller, Cheryl Misak, Jonathan Neufeld, Jon Olafsson, Phil Oliver, Jeanne Palomino, John Peterman, David Reidy, Peter Reiner, Peter Simpson, Walter Sinnott-Armstrong, Justin Snedegar, Matthew Stanley, Patricia Talisse, Paul Taylor, Rob Tempio, Miram Thalos, Jeffrey Tlumak, Larry Torcello, Rebecca Tuvel, Sarah Tyson, Kevin Vallier, Brendan Warmke, Leif Wenar, and Julian Wuerth.

I also thank those who attended presentations of this material at Dickinson College, University of Binghamton, University of Canberra, University of Colorado Denver, University of Connecticut Law School, George Mason University, Georgetown

University, University of Iceland, Pacific University, Pepperdine University, Rhodes College, Rochester Institute of Technology, Royal Holloway University, University of St. Andrews, University of Tennessee Knoxville, Wageningen University, Frist Museum of the Arts, CUNY Academy for the Humanities and Sciences, Institute for Humane Studies, and National Humanities Center.

I am especially appreciative of the continuing support and enthusiasm of Lucy Randall, Hannah Doyle, and Gabriella Baldassin of Oxford University Press. My greatest debt is to Joanne Billett. Her love, camaraderie, humor, and good sense made this book possible.

# Introduction

## The Big Picture

In 2018, I delivered a public lecture about democracy. My presentation focused on how our partisan divides have spilled over into nearly all areas of our social life, often creating rifts among friends and family members. I argued that even though these local tensions might look insignificant from the perspective of national politics, they nonetheless are dangerous for democracy. My overriding message was that we must strive to keep politics in its proper place, and we can do this by staying mindful of the fact that people are not defined by their partisan affiliation. Although the talk was about democracy, it was not an expression of any particular partisan viewpoint. I was talking about democracy, not politics.

The presentation was well received. Many approached me to convey appreciation, discuss particular details of what I had said, or ask for further information about my research. One attendee, however, stuck out from the others. An older man wearing a cowboy hat waited until most of the others had walked away. He shook my hand vigorously before saying, "I want you to know I agree with everything you just said up there." I thanked him for attending the event. He then got closer and added, "It was a surprise, you know." Intrigued, I asked him what was surprising. He replied, "Well, before coming here I looked you up. I saw that you're a philosophy professor, so I figured you'd be a Democrat." Even though he pronounced the word "Democrat" with a mild sneer that indicated his meaning, he paused for a moment and clarified, "I figured I was going to have to fight you from the audience." I honestly didn't know what to say, so I again thanked him for attending, adding that I was pleased to hear that he found the presentation interesting.

I look back on this interaction often. I'm not sure what the man meant by saying he expected to have to fight. Given his age, I doubt that the man was seriously anticipating a physical altercation. But who knows? I'm sure that he had, indeed, inferred from my profession that I would have more liberal political commitments than his own. His surprise came from the fact that, despite taking me to be a political opponent, he found himself agreeing with what I had to say about democracy. His assumption apparently had been that a Democrat would not be able to say anything worthwhile about democracy. In supposing that we embraced opposing partisan affiliations, he expected that our disagreement would be all-encompassing, total. What's more, even though I doubt he would have protested from the audience had I said something that he found objectionable, he still expected our disagreements to be worth wrangling over.

It's not clear to me what the man concluded from the fact that he found my presentation agreeable. I'd like to think he emerged from it with a renewed sense of how significant partisan divides can exist alongside an even more important consensus regarding the value of democracy itself, and why we mustn't allow our partisanship to dissolve this common ground. I hope he drew the conclusion that he could share deep political commitments with those who affiliate with an opposing party.

But there was something in the way he lingered on his statement about my being a Democrat that leads me to a different hypothesis about what he had concluded. He was prompting me to affirm a partisan identity, to state my political affiliation. I didn't oblige, but I also did not react negatively to the man's implicit affirmation that he's a Republican. I think the man may have concluded from this that I'm not a Democrat after all. I suspect he reasoned from the fact that I had spoken sensibly about democracy that we must share a political affiliation. He took our agreement about democracy to entail a consensus about politics as such. The common ground between us served as proof that we stood in the same place.

In a way, this man embodied the problem my presentation had aimed to address. He regarded my partisan affiliation as my defining feature, not only as a citizen but as a person. He thus had allowed politics to get inside his head, to colonize his thinking about all of his social interactions. He seemed, moreover, not to be fully aware that he had adopted this stance. After all, he was ascribing a partisan identity to me while also expressing agreement with a presentation that had focused on the democratic perils of seeing people strictly through the lens of partisan affiliation. While working under the assumption that I'm a Democrat, he was expecting my message to be objectionable, something to be fought against. He said he expected to have to oppose me as I was speaking, in real time. He must have walked into the lecture hall confident that he already had a good idea of what I was going to say.

This interaction is what got me thinking about the difficulty of upholding the values and ideals of democratic citizenship while confronting political opponents. Democracy requires that citizens recognize one another as political equals, partners in the shared enterprise of self-government. Recognizing others as our fellow  citizens is partly a matter of conducting ourselves in ways that manifest a due regard for their perspectives, concerns, and ideas. Citizenship thus calls us to adopt a *moral* stance. However, in certain cases, upholding this stance strikes us as naive and irresponsible. We typically see our opponents' political opinions as flawed and misguided. Moreover, it often seems to us that our opposition's commitment to democracy is itself disingenuous, at best strategic. When we uphold the norms of proper democratic citizenship that they flout, we provide them with a tactical advantage in pursuing their flawed political objectives. Why supply them with an easy route to success?

Thus, the *democrat's dilemma*. That's the term I use to capture the tension between the moral requirement to recognize the equality of political opponents and the moral directive to pursue and promote political justice. Note the lowercase *d* in the word "democrat." The democrat's dilemma does not emerge out of a partisan affiliation or political agenda. It's not the *Democrat's* dilemma. Instead, the democrat's dilemma arises for democratic citizens as such, regardless of these other features of their politics. Note also that it's a dilemma *for* democratic citizens. Although this book aims to give the democrat's dilemma a theoretical articulation and resolution, the dilemma itself emerges in the course of a citizen's political engagement. When confronting it, citizens are torn between two democratic edicts. They must find a way to navigate the conflict between them.

A common reaction to the democrat's dilemma needs to be addressed straightaway. It might seem that the dilemma admits of an easy response. One might contend that democracy is for authentic citizens who uphold democratic norms in a reciprocal spirit. Thus, when we are dealing with opponents whose democratic commitments are only nominal, we should suspend our own democratic commitments, striving instead to prevail so that democracy might be preserved. Anything less is itself a kind of betrayal of democracy. Consequently, when it comes to high-stakes politics, it seems that we have sufficient reason to suspend democratic relations with our opponents, to treat them not as fellow citizens but instead as obstacles. The dilemma hence resolves in favor of justice.

This looks like a simple but decisive resolution to the democrat's dilemma. However, there is less to it than meets the eye. The ordinary and otherwise praiseworthy activities of democratic citizenship expose us to forces that systematically distort our conception of our political opposition. These forces lead us to over-ascribe extreme views, sinister dispositions, and corrupt intentions to rivals.

Our opponents, of course, are driven by similar forces. They thus see us and our allies in a similar light.

As a result, the citizenry segregates into opposed partisan camps, with those in each camp regarding the members of the others as insufficiently invested in democracy and therefore undeserving of the kind of treatment appropriate among democratic citizens. In the end, when we adopt the simple resolution of the democrat's dilemma, we are driven into the stance that democracy is not possible among citizens who disagree about politics. Yet that's to say that democracy simply is not possible, full stop. The simple resolution is a surrender.

This book is about the challenge of upholding the kind of political relations appropriate among democratic citizens amid political struggles involving opponents whose views strike us as misguided, ignorant, and even repugnant. I call this the challenge of *sustaining democracy*. I take it that the challenge is familiar among politically active democratic citizens. Observe, however, that the challenge has at least two dimensions. The first can be captured in a question about our obligations: *why should we* sustain democracy with our foes? The second reflects a more practical question of what steps we can take to preserve within ourselves the necessary attitudes and dispositions: *how can we* sustain democracy with them? One aim of this book is to show that sustaining democracy is more challenging than it seems.

The challenge owes partly to the fact that under the political circumstances where citizens are most likely to feel the pinch of the democrat's dilemma, they often have compelling reasons to *suspend* democracy rather than sustain it. I will argue that although these reasons are indeed weighty, they are not as decisive as they typically appear. Showing this will require a careful inspection of certain features of democratic citizenship. Before launching into this kind of detailed examination, though, we need to see the big picture.

## 1. Common Ground and Its Erosion

Let's take the matter up from square one. Democracy's success depends upon an active citizenry. Yet when citizens engage together in politics, they quickly discover that they disagree with one another. These disagreements tend to run deep. They can reflect opposing ideas about the nature and purposes of democracy itself. Consequently, political disagreements are persistent and often unpleasant. Yet they are to be expected. Political disagreements are the upshots of the freedom and equality that democracy secures for its citizens. In order for democracy to function well, then, citizens must work together amid their political differences. We might say that we need to partner in the shared task of democracy *despite* those differences.

Much of the architecture of democracy is designed to manage political divisions. Open and frequent elections, freedom of expression, accountable representatives, transparent government, and equality under the law all are institutions that make it possible for citizens to live together peacefully even though they are divided over how the political world ought to be. The fairness and transparency of these democratic mechanisms enable citizens to lose an election without thereby losing their status as equal participants in the collective endeavor of democracy.

Democracy is rooted in a hard truth: when it comes to politics, you can't always get what you want. If society is going to be relatively just and stable, we have to live alongside others who espouse opposing viewpoints about what's best. More than this, we have to recognize that they are our fellow citizens, each entitled to an equal say despite their flawed political views. The hope—and it is only a hope—is that when citizens' political disputes are conducted by means of democratic processes, our equality is preserved, and politics goes better for everyone.

I suspect that this depiction of democracy will strike my reader as agreeable, perhaps even obvious. The idea that democracy thrives when it is driven by the energetic participation of citizens embracing a broad and inclusive variety of conflicting viewpoints is popular across the political spectrum. So, too, is the claim that democracy founders when political differences are suppressed, marginalized, or disallowed. Despite our deep political divides, all sides tend to agree that democracy runs on open and honest political engagement across differences. We grant that there needs to be political exchange if democratic government is to be accountable to its citizens. Moreover, properly democratic engagement among proponents of conflicting ideas is a fundamental way in which citizens recognize one another as equal partners in democracy. This much is common ground for a democracy.[1]

Yet in the United States and elsewhere, citizens are growing more disposed to regard their political opponents not only as mistaken or misguided, but also as positively threatening and dangerous.[2] We increasingly tend to see political ideas that oppose our own as inconsistent with the basic commitments of democracy. Even minor deviations from what we regard as politically proper are frequently amplified into wholesale violations of democracy itself. Although we hold our beliefs about our opponents—their ideas, values, and lifestyles—with intensifying confidence, we actually don't understand them well.[3] And, as one might expect, we misunderstand our opponents in ways that exaggerate their flaws. We over-ascribe to them extreme views, intolerant attitudes, crooked dispositions, inept thinking habits, and malevolent intentions.

That's bad news for democracy. Productive political interaction across differences calls for citizens to recognize one another as fellow democratic participants, rather than as threats to democracy as such. This means that citizens need to be able to recognize a field of *good-faith* political disagreement, a range of views that oppose their own but are nonetheless consistent with democracy's fundamental principles. Moreover, citizens must be able to recognize that at least *some* of their opponents hold political views of that kind: wrong, yet not antidemocratic; misguided, but consistent with democratic values. And, of course, citizens need to be able to treat those whom they take to be in the wrong as their fellow citizens. Amid political division, citizens must uphold the democratic common ground. Otherwise, democracy is jeopardized.

Here's some more bad news: the troubling attitudes mentioned a moment ago thrive among citizens who regard themselves as politically active. In fact, these attitudes are stimulated *by* political engagement.[4] The more politically active we are, the more prone we become to seeing our opponents as threats to be neutralized rather than as fellow citizens to be cooperated with. Still, democracy flourishes only when citizens are active participants. Thus, a puzzle: a politically active citizenry is necessary for democracy's success and yet can subvert it. Engaged citizenship makes democracy work but also can erode the common ground that makes democracy possible. When politics gets inside our heads, we can grow less capable of democratic citizenship. The democrat's dilemma is an occupational hazard, so to speak. It's baked into our job as citizens.

## 2. Is Democracy Self-Defeating?

Democracy can be imperiled by our earnest acts of citizenship. Really? The thought may strike you as absurd. This is because we tend to think that democracy's troubles almost always stem from a failure on the part of citizens to live up to democracy's demands. For example, many say that political corruption is possible because citizens don't pay enough attention to what elected officials do. We also commonly attribute bad electoral outcomes to citizens' ignorance, selfishness, or shortsightedness. "Special interests" rush in where citizens can't be bothered to tread. When citizens fall short, democracy suffers.

Yes, a good deal of what goes wrong in democratic politics owes to failures of proper citizenship. Democratic citizens indeed must take responsibility for their politics. However, it is common to infer from this that *all* of democracy's dysfunctions owe to citizens' falling down on the job. Many conclude that every one of democracy's problems is best addressed by enhanced citizen participation. Two of the greatest democratic thinkers of the twentieth century, Jane Addams and John Dewey, put it well: the cure for democracy's ills is always more democracy. Here *more* means *better* and *more authentic*. Accordingly, the thought at the heart of this book, that democratic participation itself could give rise to a distinctive kind of political pathology, seems confused.

But it's not at all confused. Instead, the Addams/Dewey slogan is wrong. Democracy can break down even when every citizen is an active, sincere, and conscientious participant. There are unique dysfunctions that befall democracy *because* citizens are authentically engaged in politics. Democracy can be endangered from *within* by citizens who are taking the enterprise of self-government seriously and acting roughly, as they should. In a nutshell, some of democracy's ills are caused by citizens' sincere and earnest political activity. More democratic participation can't cure those ills.

It might seem obvious that more participation makes for better democratic politics. Yet I will argue that earnest democratic participation exposes citizens to forces that can subvert their capacity to recognize the political equality of their opponents. The dissolution of this capacity leads to a breakdown of democracy itself. There's something of a paradox afoot. One might say that democratic citizenship could be *self-defeating*.

The possibility that democratic citizenship is self-defeating has been underappreciated among democratic theorists. Consequently, the opening two chapters aim to formulate the problem precisely. As I see it, the difficulty emerges from the conflict between two moral requirements of democratic citizenship: the requirement to pursue justice and the requirement to acknowledge the political equality of one's fellow citizens. When caught in the democrat's dilemma, the citizen looks for reasons to uphold her commitment to regarding her foes as her equals. She seeks a reason to sustain democracy.

We can grasp the democrat's dilemma more clearly by considering a conceptual point that will be emphasized in Chapter 1. Democracy is an ideal of political equality, a vision of politics as self-government among equals. In this sense, democracy is centrally a *moral* proposal and aspiration. As is commonly observed, in a democracy the government must treat its people as political equals, as properly *citizens* rather than merely its *subjects*. It is somewhat less frequently noted, however, that this requirement applies *among* citizens as well. As democratic citizens, *we* are required to recognize our fellow citizens as *our* political equals. They're to be regarded as equal partners in the collective project of self-government. Among other things, their equality means that they do not merely *get* an equal say in political decision-making, but are *entitled* to one. Democracy demands that we acknowledge that entitlement.

Now here's the rub. It's easy to regard our political allies as our equals. But this requirement applies also to those citizens whom we count as our political adversaries. They are our political equals, too. We are required to treat them as such, even though we may also despise their views and perhaps consider them to be advocates of injustice. What's more, when they prevail politically, we must acknowledge that legitimate government is required to enact their will, despite the fact that we see their views as inconsistent with justice. And even when they fail at the polls, we must regard it as legitimate for them to continue to campaign, critique, protest, and lobby on behalf of a political agenda that we may regard as unconscionable, even unjust. In short, recognizing the political equality of our fellow citizens calls us not only to sometimes assess it as legitimate for our government to implement what we see as injustice, but also to regard it as right for government to protect the voices and political efforts of those who advocate for policies that we regard as unjust.

This formulation is too rough. As it stands, it lacks crucial details. For one thing, there are limits to what democratic citizens must respect and tolerate, just as there are limits to what democratic government can enact. There are also limits to what citizens may do in protesting policies they find objectionable. Furthermore, democracy never requires us to simply *acquiesce* in or *accede* to the views of our opposition; recognizing their equality is consistent with abhorring their political views. More generally, though, the requirement as stated does not adequately spell out what it means to regard our fellow citizens as our equals. What kind of political conduct is required of us, given that we must recognize the political equality of our fellow citizens?

These nuances will be introduced in Chapter 2. For now, be assured that even once the necessary distinctions are included, regarding our political opponents as our equals will still be a challenge. Democracy asks a lot.

Note that this demand is *moral*. Democracy says that we owe to our fellow citizens a certain kind of regard, and a corresponding manner of conduct, even when we see their political views as severely misguided and possibly unjust. As indicated earlier, part of recognizing our opponents' political equality involves acknowledging their *entitlement* to an equal share of political power. Hence democracy requires us to embrace a political order that, within certain broad constraints, gives equal power to truth and error, justice and injustice.

In other contexts, we say that the prescribed arrangement demands moral *complicity*. In a democracy, however, even though citizens are called upon to *take responsibility* for their government by standing up for justice as they see it, they must also recognize the political equality of those who would enact injustice. Such is the oddly conflicted moral stance that constitutes a central virtue of the democratic citizen. We might say that democracy not only is demanding, but also foists upon citizens a *moral burden*. This burden lies at the heart of the democrat's dilemma. It's what makes sustaining democracy such a challenge.

I recognize that this depiction remains too blunt. The account will be sharpened in the chapters to come. Thus far, my point simply has been that, even at its best, democracy is not easy. Its difficulty owes partly to the moral burden of recognizing the equality of our political opponents, even when we assess them as advocating injustice.

That democracy is difficult in this way is old news. Recall, however, that this book is addressed to a problem having to do with self-defeat. To repeat, my claim is that authentic democratic participation can imperil democracy by eroding our capacity to regard our opponents in the required way. To get a better sense of how this might be so, we will need to examine the cognitive phenomenon known as *belief polarization*. This is the focus of Chapter 3.

Belief polarization is uncommonly robust. It drives members of like-minded groups to shift into more extreme versions of themselves. When belief is polarized, group members become more fervent and more confident advocates of the group's identity and ideas. They also become more dismissive of opposing views, as well as more disposed to demean and distrust those who hold them. In severe cases, belief polarization leads us to regard those outside of our group as irrational, inscrutable, depraved, and threatening. Belief polarization thus undermines our ability to regard our political opponents as our equals.

Yet that's not all. Belief polarization also negatively impacts our relations with our allies. As like-minded groups undergo belief polarization, their members not only become more extreme, but also become more *alike* to one another. This is because belief polarization intensifies pressures to conform to group expectations. As a group polarizes, its members also come to adopt more exacting standards of *authentic* group membership. Consequently, strategies for detecting poseurs and fakers multiply. Minor deviations from group norms are magnified into signals of sweeping betrayal, while doctrinal purity is valorized. Moreover, as belief-polarized groups become more invested in conformity among their membership, they also become less tolerant of deviation, less self-critical, and increasingly hierarchical. In short, belief polarization leads like-minded groups to expel members and thus to shrink. This naturally serves to undercut the democratic efficacy of our political coalitions.

Now for the crucial point. As was mentioned earlier, otherwise laudable forms of democratic engagement *heighten* our exposure to belief polarization. Hence the problem of self-defeat: earnest democratic participation can lead us to *fail* at responsible democratic citizenship. It can make us worse citizens and less effective political agents, which in turn leads us to become unwitting contributors to broader political dysfunctions. Sustaining democracy may be even harder than we normally recognize.

Be assured that this is not an antidemocracy book. The upshot is not that democracy requires so much of us that it should be replaced with some alternative arrangement. The lesson instead is that one of democracy's underappreciated strengths is that it calls upon citizens to scrutinize their own political thinking. Democracy requires us specifically to reflect on our vulnerabilities as citizens—to recognize our (and our allies') susceptibility to belief polarization and to take steps to try to mitigate it.

More generally, the positive message of this book is that democracy requires *maintenance*. In one sense, that's old news, too. It is commonplace to acknowledge that democratic institutions need regular assessment, revision, expansion, and reform. According to many well-developed theories, democracy *simply is* the ongoing project of revitalizing democracy's institutions and practices.

But I will propose that democracy also calls for a different sort of maintenance. Democracy requires us to manage belief polarization, the force *within ourselves* that is activated by earnest political engagement and that dismantles our ability to behave as citizens should. Given this, we must work hard to preserve within ourselves the attitudes and dispositions that are proper for democratic citizens. In short, sustaining democracy is not only a matter of upholding proper civic relations with our political opponents; it also involves inward-looking self-regulation, and thus self-critique.

Although this is a philosophy book about democratic citizenship, it also is a book *for* democratic citizens. It articulates a view of how we should conduct ourselves politically, especially when we are dealing with political foes. But it does this with eyes wide open. For one thing, the argument recognizes that political conflict is endemic to democracy. I will *not* be arguing that proper citizenship demands that we learn to love our political opponents or set aside our political rivalries. Rather, I will argue that we *should* sustain democracy, even when the stakes are high. Even in the pinch, so to speak.

In my view, the democrat's dilemma is well-motivated. We often have *good reason* to *suspend* our commitment to the political equality of our opponents. There are cases where treating our foes as our equals reduces the chance of achieving our political aims. Insofar as we see our aims as just and those of our opposition as unjust, it is reasonable to raise the question of *why we should sustain democracy*. Why not simply forget about the standard of regard and conduct that democracy requires of us, and fight for what's right? Why should we strive to uphold democratic relations with our opposition, given the moral stakes and their apparent cravenness?

In other words, this book treats sustaining democracy as more than a difficult practical assignment. It recognizes that the democrat's dilemma is a moral problem that emerges out of the endeavor to take democratic citizenship seriously. My contention is that although there are indeed instances in which the political stakes are such that we have compelling moral reasons to suspend our democratic commitments for the sake of achieving our ends, these reasons are very rarely conclusive. In fact, I will argue that the phenomenon of belief polarization leads us to overestimate the weight of the reasons we have to suspend our democratic commitments. More positively, my view is that insofar as we care about achieving justice, we generally ought to sustain democracy, even when the moral stakes are high.

However, as I have already suggested, the argument does not rest solely upon an account of what we owe to our political foes. To be clear, we ordinarily *do* owe them the kind of regard that is appropriate among equals. Yet, again, this is not a "love your enemies" book. I will argue that we also owe it to our *political allies* to treat our *political opponents* as our equals. This is because, due to belief polarization, when we decline to sustain democracy in the case of our foes, we also damage our ability to regard our allies as our equals. This in turn often undermines our political objectives. In other words, when we decline to sustain democracy with our adversaries, we imperil our political alliances and disserve our political ends. The result is that we should sustain democracy, even when the chips are down.

By the close of Chapter 3, we will have seen that belief polarization both supplies an account of a central mechanism driving the democrat's dilemma and points us in the direction of distinctive reasons for sustaining democracy. The argument for *why* we should sustain democracy with our political opponents thus will be complete at that point. However, sustaining our capacity to regard our opponents as our equals remains a tall order. Are we up to the task?

Chapter 4 takes up the question of *how we can* sustain democracy. There, I will explore some strategies for productive political engagement across sharp partisan divides. I will argue that although these may be helpful as far as they go, they are ultimately insufficient. The defect with these strategies is that they're too tightly focused on face-to-face engagement organized around pro-and-con discussion of the policies over which political foes are divided. Interaction of this kind might be suitable for political exchange among citizens who are not yet in the grip of belief polarization. But in the case of polarized citizens, this format can exacerbate divisions. If we want to take steps to sustain democracy, we must look elsewhere.

I will recommend a two-part strategy. First, citizens must recognize their vulnerability to belief polarization. This requires them to locate and grapple with *reasonable criticisms* of their political opinions. Note that this prescription does not call for citizens to more regularly debate with their opponents the pros and cons of their conflicting proposals; rather, the idea is to focus on the opposition's *criticisms* of one's own commitments. This helps one to keep in mind that one's political views can be *improved*: more clearly articulated, more compellingly supported. In turn, this realization serves to remind us that there is a scope of acceptable variation in political opinion, even among our allies. For reasons that will be explained, these interventions can be expected to ease, or at least not activate, belief polarization within ourselves and our alliances. And, to put the point bluntly, managing belief polarization is more than half of the task of sustaining democracy. Perhaps it is the entire task.

The second step in sustaining democracy is to secure the conditions under which the first step can be activated. I will argue that in order to manage belief polarization, citizens need to establish *political distance* between themselves and their fellow citizens, allies and adversaries alike. They need *occasionally* to step back from the fray of partisan politics and engage in political reflection. We tend to think of democratic citizenship, and political engagement in general, nearly strictly in terms of group-based public behavior. Part of my proposal for sustaining democracy claims that there are also modes of political action that require solitude.

The argument is completed in Chapter 4. I will have laid out accounts of why we should sustain democracy and how we can go about doing so. The Epilogue returns briefly to the big picture, to the wider ideal of democracy as a self-governing society of equal citizens. From that perspective, we will see that when it comes to democratic politics, what we owe to the other side is to be a good ally to those on our own.

## 3. Sustaining Democracy and Overdoing Democracy

This book is a sequel to my 2019 book, *Overdoing Democracy*. As I see it, this book takes up a crucial issue that its predecessor occasions but does not address. It might help, then, to close this Introduction with a brief discussion of how the argument of the current book fits with the earlier work. Readers who are unfamiliar with *Overdoing Democracy*, or who are not interested in the relationship between the two books, may now skip ahead to Chapter 1.

In *Overdoing Democracy*, I argued that when the whole of social life is saturated with politics, our exposure to belief polarization is intensified, and this leads to the erosion of the moral capacities we need in order to enact democracy well. The capacities in question are those we need in order to regard our political opposition as nonetheless our political equals, fellow citizens who are entitled to an equal say. In short, by overdoing democracy we obstruct our capacity to regard our fellow citizens as our democratic equals and thus contribute to the erosion of democracy.

The result of this is escalating *civic enmity*, the condition under which we are unable to see our political rivals as capable and deserving of democratic citizenship. Under such conditions, citizens regard one another as either allies or obstacles, and democracy devolves into a cold civil war among mutually inscrutable tribes. The argument of *Overdoing Democracy* thus is "outward-looking." It is focused on the moral capacities necessary for treating our political opponents as our equals.

This argument prompts the issue to which the present book is directed. Given that our opponents seem to us to be committed to odious political views and insufficiently committed to democratic norms, why do we owe it to them to try to uphold properly democratic relations with them? Why not embrace the conclusion that regardless of what the democratic *ideal* prescribes, real-world democracy is *politics*, and politics is at best a cold civil war? That's the democrat's dilemma.

*Sustaining Democracy* addresses this dilemma by developing an *inward-looking* argument demonstrating why it is crucial to sustain our democratic commitments, even in the midst of political opponents who seem only nominally committed to democracy. As I emphasized earlier, the core of the argument has to do with a feature of belief polarization that was not addressed in *Overdoing Democracy*—namely, that as groups polarize, they become *internally* more homogeneous, more intensely demanding of in-group conformity across an expanding range of behaviors, and thus increasingly hierarchical. In other words, belief polarization leads us to become unable to tolerate differences *among our allies*. Accepting differences among our allies is necessary both for preserving the democratic nature of our group and for optimizing the group's democratic efficacy.

*Overdoing Democracy* made the case that if we wish to perform well as democratic citizens, we need sometimes to engage together in cooperative activities that are nonpolitical. Such activities are necessary if we are to manage belief polarization. This argument leaves open the obvious question of how, given the forces of political saturation and belief polarization, we should conduct ourselves when engaged in politics. This is the question to be addressed here. Once again, managing belief polarization is the central task. In a nutshell, the perhaps surprising conclusion is that we should sustain democratic relations with our political opponents because if we do not, we damage our capacity to treat our friends as our political equals. More precisely, in failing to sustain democracy, we succumb to forces that transform our political friends into political enemies.

## 4. Final Preliminaries

Before beginning in earnest, a few additional comments are in order. I mentioned earlier that this is a book *for* democratic citizens in that it attempts to take seriously the challenges of citizenship as they arise in the real world of democratic politics. But there's an additional sense in which the book is for citizens: I have endeavored to *write for* citizens. I have tried to set aside the trappings of academic writing. The book presupposes no prior knowledge of democratic theory and is, I hope, largely jargon-free. Experimental results are presented in narrative or anecdotal formats, without use of charts or mathematics. Technical points have been relegated to the endnotes, as have references to the relevant scholarly literature. Readers who want to follow up on the philosophical niceties of the argument should consult the endnotes; those who are not concerned with these particulars may simply ignore them.

Still, this is an academic book. It will sometimes be necessary to linger on details and distinctions that some readers might find tedious. My acknowledgment that there are occasions of this kind certainly does nothing to make them more bearable, but I hope it may encourage readers to see them as unavoidable.

One last point. My argument draws upon empirical data. These data are typically indexed to the United States. A good deal of the relevant research has to do with the United States, where the trends I will be examining are especially pronounced. However, these phenomena are not *exclusive* to that country. The difficulties I will be discussing reflect certain vulnerabilities of democracy as such. Although not every democracy suffers from the dysfunctions I will document in this book, every democracy is vulnerable to them.

# 1

# Democracy as a Society of Equals

Not very long ago, I was seated next to an outgoing stranger at a wedding. We got to chatting and eventually she asked my occupation. I replied that I'm a political theorist. This provoked a reaction that suggested that she took me to be a political consultant or strategist. I explained that I do not work in politics, but rather am a professor specializing in the philosophy of democracy. She responded, "What's *philosophical* about democracy?"

My answer to her question must have been welcoming, since we spent the better half of the evening talking spiritedly about a range of questions: What does it mean for the people to govern themselves? Are citizens too ignorant to cast meaningful votes? Why is there a voting age? What can be done about widespread public disinformation campaigns? Are term limits inconsistent with popular rule? Are future generations entitled to a voice in current political decision-making? Should corporations be treated as citizens?

In the course of our conversation, I learned that before taking up her current profession, she worked in politics in Washington, DC. This explained why she had detailed views about many of the issues we discussed. However, at the end of the evening she said, "You know, I had no idea people were still trying to figure all that stuff out." She went on to explain that while she was working in Washington, the assumption was that all of the conceptual issues about democracy had been resolved long ago, and that all that remained as far as *thinking* about democracy goes is strategizing about how to advance one's political agenda.

I suspect this attitude still prevails in Washington. But my companion's remark points to a more general hurdle that one faces when writing about democracy for a general readership. For those living in a democracy, politics is pervasive. So it's easy to lose sight of the fact that the entire enterprise raises philosophical questions that are as yet not fully resolved. We often bring to political discussions tacit assumptions about what democracy is all about, views that we tend to treat as long settled. The suggestion that fundamental questions about democracy are still worth exploring raises suspicions. As is often the case in philosophy, making the case that there's a question worth asking is the first task.

Here's a case in point. This book tries to address a familiar but undertheorized problem facing democratic citizens, the *democrat's dilemma*. In formulating that problem, I will claim that certain admirable modes of democratic engagement can erode our ability to perform well as citizens. This claim is likely to strike readers as obviously confused. How can a form of political engagement be both commendable and damaging from the democratic point of view? Some may regard the problem at the heart of this book as a nonstarter.

A lot turns on what *democracy* means. In order to grasp the problem that I aim to address, we need to begin there. Specifically, we need to see that democracy is not simply a form of government or a process for making group decisions, but rather a kind of society in which citizens govern together as equals. This chapter spells out that view of democracy.

Although the formula might sound simple, the idea of a self-governing society of equals is complicated. The important nuances will be captured in the chapter's three main parts. The first establishes that democracy is fundamentally a *moral idea* of political equality. The second part explains how this moral idea gives rise to a democratic *ethos* of citizenship, a set of requirements for citizens to perform certain tasks and embody certain virtues. In the third part of this chapter, I argue that democracy is best understood as a kind of ideal—a *practical ideal*, I will call it—that identifies a social aspiration and provides a basis for political criticism.

This may seem a lot to tackle. However, the task is lighter than it might appear. The account that is developed will strike familiar tones among democratic theorists and citizens alike. To some, the account may seem so familiar as to be boilerplate. This is by design. I hope that most of what I have to say will strike readers as noncontroversial, perhaps even obvious.

I aim to begin from a conception of democracy that is robust and yet ordinary, a view that largely steers clear of current debates among democratic theorists. This will help to show that the problem that this book addresses—the democrat's dilemma—is general rather than a product of my particular conception of democracy. The focused articulation of the problem is the task of Chapters 2 and 3. For now, the task is to provide a substantive, but nonetheless conventional, view of democracy and its value. In this sense, the current chapter lays out rudiments, the basic elements upon which the book's central argument will be built.

## 1.  Democracy as a Moral Idea

We commonly think of democracy in simple terms. We say it is a form of government where the people rule. This naturally prompts the question of what it means for the people to rule. In response, we usually focus on what might be democracy's most distinctive institution: the election. We say that in a democracy, the people rule in that they make political decisions by means of voting in elections. Of course, we recognize that the people rule by way of an elaborate system of representation. It's ultimately politicians and their appointees who make decisions. Still, elections place people in political office. One could say, then, that our popular view of democracy is *institutional*, or, in light of its particular focus, *electoral*.

That we tend to think of democracy in this way is not surprising. Elections are indeed distinctively democratic instruments for decision-making. Some would go so far as to say that elections are among democracy's *defining* features. Although some philosophers have offered compelling arguments for thinking that public lotteries and similar arrangements are suitably democratic alternatives to elections, we nonetheless tend to see elections as the *default* instrument of self-government among equals.[1]

In any case, elections probably loom larger in the political life of the citizen than any other characteristically democratic institution. Elections are so central to our view of democracy that in everyday contexts we say we're being "democratic" when we propose to make a decision by taking a vote. The electoral conception is popular because it's true to our political experience.

The electoral conception of democracy is fine as far as it goes. The trouble is that it doesn't go very far. Thinking of democracy strictly in terms of elections raises the question of *why* that particular institution is central. If one responds that elections are vital because democracy is the rule of the people, we're returned to where we started. What does it mean for the people to rule? Although it is intuitive, there's less to the electoral view of democracy than meets the eye.

The electoral view is inadequate because democracy's institutions—even its *defining* institutions—are devised to fulfill a purpose, to serve an objective. In order to understand them, we need to ask what they're for, what they're supposed to achieve. We therefore must look beyond democracy's characteristic institutions. Perhaps it would be better to say that we need to look *underneath* them, to discover their underlying point.

We begin to see the underpinnings of these familiar institutions by noticing that when we talk about elections, we almost always refer to decision-making processes that are *fair* and *open*. We think that an election where only some of the votes are counted, where some with the entitlement to vote are prevented from doing so, or where only one candidate is permitted is no election at all. In other words, in order for an election to count as *democratic*, it must be structured in a way that gives everyone an equal say.[2]

It may seem too obvious to be worth stating, but the very idea of an election embeds the idea that everyone who is affected by a collective decision is entitled to an equal share of the decision-making power. Elections and the other familiar institutions of democracy therefore serve a *moral idea*, a conception of who is entitled to what. To understand democracy, we need to begin there.

Democracy is based in the moral idea of political equality. In this context, equality does not mean uniformity. Democracy is not the idea that we're all the same, equally admirable and meritorious, or in some other sense interchangeable. Rather, democracy is the proposition that a stable and decent society can be maintained in the absence of lords, masters, sovereigns, superiors, and kings. Democracy is the rejection of political hierarchy.

But democracy doesn't stop there. It is also the view that monarchy, aristocracy, and other such hierarchical arrangements are *unjust* because they are inconsistent with our equality. Democracy thus also claims that such forms of government are illegitimate, unentitled to rule.

Yet the democratic idea of political equality does more than debunk hierarchical forms of politics. It also prescribes a positive view of government. In a democracy, the people are not merely the government's *subjects*. Government does not simply rule over them. Rather, the people are properly *citizens*, equals who share political power in a system of self-government. This means that democratic government serves its citizens rather than the other way around. It means that democratic government is *accountable* to its citizens. Its job is to enact their will. When it fails to do so, the citizens have a rightful complaint to which government must respond. More generally, when democratic government acts, it must be prepared to *answer* to the people, to respond to their criticisms and justify itself. Should government prove unable or unwilling to do so, it loses its claim to legitimacy and faces morally justified rebellion.

We now can see why certain institutions are so central to democracy. Elections are instruments by which citizens express their will,

instruct their representatives, and hold their government accountable. Yet note also that in a democracy, elections are not simply a
matter of casting a vote on Election Day. Elections are preceded by
campaigns, and campaigns involve a great deal of talking. In fact,
democracy proceeds largely by way of discussion, which is necessary if citizens are going to hold their government accountable.
Other defining democratic institutions—including a free press,
freedom of speech and assembly, and freedoms of conscience—all
serve to facilitate the kind of open discussion that is required for
citizens to rule themselves as political equals.

There is much more to say about these aspects of democracy.
The point thus far is that in order to understand democracy, we
need to identify the underlying moral idea that animates its basic
institutions. That idea is political equality.

## 2. Democracy as an Ethos

We have seen how the democratic idea of political equality
structures the relation between government and its citizens. Yet
political equality extends beyond the relationship between citizens
and their government. Citizens also are equal with respect to one
another; they are one another's equals. The idea of political equality
thus applies no less to the associations among citizens than to those
among citizens and the government. Political equality is not only
*vertical*; it is also *horizontal*.

To be clear, democratic citizens need not be regarded as equals
in all spheres of life. In workplaces, congregations, families, military units, and various other kinds of association there are the familiar hierarchies of bosses and employees, clergy and laypeople,
parents and children, commanding officers and the rank-and-file,
and so on. Still, no matter how things might stand with respect to
these other facets of their lives, when it comes to politics at least,
no citizen is another's subordinate, pawn, superior, or boss. No

citizen is entitled to call the shots for another, to dictate to them what they must think or how they must deploy their share of political power. In matters of politics, democratic citizens look each other in the eye.[3]

Even though no one gets to boss another around about political matters, citizens are *responsible to* one another. They are, after all, equal partners in a cooperative endeavor whose success is mutually beneficial. They therefore have obligations to one another. Moreover, their political interactions thus must reflect the fact that they are equals, each sharing responsibility for democracy. They must behave in ways that express an appropriate regard for the equal political status of their fellow citizens.

The democratic moral idea of political equality hence gives rise to certain standards of conduct. We can refer to these standards collectively as democracy's *ethos*. It is an ethos in that it involves moral standards for citizens, standards that supply a basis for praise and blame, admiration and reproach. Yet it is also *public* in that, insofar as possible, the requirements it identifies apply to individuals understood *as citizens*. That is, the ethos does not specify moral requirements for persons as such. In a democratic society, the larger questions about what makes a human life good, valuable, meaningful, or proper are generally left to the individual conscience. These are questions to be addressed by religion or philosophy in its broadest sense, not politics. Although the expectation is that the requirements of democratic citizenship will be compatible with the comprehensive moral systems that citizens may adopt, the ethos of democracy sets a moral standard of conduct for persons *in their role* as citizens only.

This ethos comprises both duties and virtues. Duties and virtues are distinct moral categories. They work in different evaluative registers, one might say. Duties specify certain acts that must be performed (or omitted), while virtues are commendable character traits. Failing to satisfy a duty typically is wrong; it renders one blameworthy and perhaps liable to sanction. Falling short of a virtue, however, is not so much *wrong* as *bad*; it renders one re-proachable, nonadmirable, and possibly corrupt. Given this dis-tinction, my claim is that democracy's idea of political equality gives rise to a view of the actions that citizens must perform (duties) and the sensibility—the dispositions and attitudes—that they must embody (virtues). Satisfying the requisite duties and manifesting the appropriate virtues are required for showing due regard for the equality of our fellow citizens. Democracy's ethos hence sets a standard for proper citizenship.

## 2.1. Duties of Citizenship

Begin with our duties as citizens. The central consideration is straightforward: one way in which citizens acknowledge one another's political equality is by doing their fair share of the work of democracy. After all, democracy requires effort. Elections must be held, offices must be filled, laws must be passed, criminal trials must be conducted, institutions and infrastructure must be maintained, and so on. In short, democracy is a group endeavor, and those who are citizens of a functioning democracy but do not contribute to it thereby free-ride on the political labor of others. Free-riding is a way of using others as a mere resource for one's own purposes. It therefore involves placing oneself above others. By free-riding, one fails to regard one's fellow citizens as equal; one disrespects their equal status.

Consequently, the democratic ethos includes a range of duties. These are requirements to contribute one's share to making democ-racy work by participating in the collective tasks without which it could not persist. As citizens, our duties include the familiar po-litical actions that we recognize an obligation to perform. For ex-ample, we tend to think that voting, serving on a jury when called to do so, and paying taxes are things that citizens ought to do. We also acknowledge that, within certain constraints, citizens are under a general obligation to obey and uphold the law, and to defend the country.

This list of the duties of citizenship is not exhaustive. A complete account would include duties associated with reporting crime and cooperating with criminal investigations and prosecutions, perhaps by serving as a witness in a trial. Furthermore, there is a duty to report, challenge, or otherwise call attention to political corruption, to be a whistle-blower. To these one might add duties to aid, assist, or rescue citizens who are in various kinds of danger, what are sometimes called *Samaritan* duties. There may also be related duties to occasionally volunteer or contribute to charitable organizations and the like. Arguably, as theorists of civil disobedience contend, citizens also have a duty to stand up to certain forms of social injustice, even at considerable personal expense. Perhaps there are conditions under which it is also a citizen's duty to stand for political office and serve if elected.

We need not attempt a full account of the duties of citizenship. Remember the narrow scope of the current argument. The point is to register a narrow, and I should think noncontroversial, thought: the duties of citizenship identify the actions it is necessary to perform if one is to contribute one's fair share to the collective project of maintaining a democratic society. Contributing one's fair share to the common endeavor is a way of *taking responsibility* for one's democracy, and this is a necessary part of respecting the political equality of one's fellow citizens.

Accordingly, when a citizen fails to satisfy these duties, she does wrong and therefore renders herself liable to criticism. There are circumstances, of course, where such failures are *excusable*, in which case criticism may be inappropriate. More importantly, not all of the duties of citizenship are equally weighty. In many democracies, neglecting to vote is considered a relatively minor dereliction—occasioning a modest fine, or simply the disapprobation of others—while other failures are treated as criminal offenses. Again, these complexities needn't detain us. My point is simply that failing to satisfy the duties of citizenship constitutes some degree of wrongdoing. The wrong is committed against one's fellow citizens.

Yet this does not capture the full import of our political equality. In performing the duties of citizenship, we contribute our fair share to the collective endeavor of democracy and therefore avoid *disrespecting* fellow citizens. But respecting others as our equals is not simply a matter of omitting behavior that disrespects them. Treating fellow citizens as our equals has a *positive* dimension as well. We are required not merely to avoid violating the equality of our fellow citizens; we must also *acknowledge* them as equals.

To do so, we must perform the duties of citizenship with a certain *temperament* or *sensibility*. We must bring to our political behavior the dispositions and attitudes that are appropriate for an individual who is engaged in a cooperative endeavor of self-government among equals. In short, in order to complete our picture of what it takes for citizens to regard each other as equals, we need to devise a conception of the virtues of citizenship.

## 2.2.  Virtues of Citizenship

To see more clearly why a conception of virtue is needed, we must take a step back. Although democracy is self-government among equals, it nonetheless involves exercises of coercive power by some over others. In this respect, democracy is like all modes of politics. The difference is that democracy involves the claim that its exercises of coercive power are consistent with the political equality of those who are coerced. In other words, democracy is the proposition that you can be forced to accede to rules that you reject, yet retain your status as an equal. It is the claim that there's a kind of coercive force that's not mere *bullying*. That idea might strike you as puzzling. It *should*.

In order to think this through, we need to bring the puzzle into sharper focus. Observe that unanimity is seldom required in order to make a legitimate political decision in a democracy. Although decision rules vary, in most democratic contexts, all that is needed for a decision to be reached is a *plurality* of votes. When a democracy decides, then, some get the result they favor, while others are expected to comply with a result that they did not support. Should those who do oppose the prevailing outcome decline to comply, they render themselves liable to sanction. In fact, we think that democratic government is *right* to force compliance.

Democratic citizens thus are sometimes required to comply with results and decisions that they do not support and might see as objectionable. On such occasions they are coerced, forced to abide by policies that they would otherwise reject. As this coercion is directed by the political activity of their fellow citizens, they are hence forced to obey the collective will of others. This looks like a simple case of subordination—some call the shots for others and compliance is enforced. Democracy claims that coercion of this kind is legitimate, so long as it is the product of democratic processes. The puzzle is how this arrangement could possibly be consistent with the claim that citizens are political equals.

Full exploration of this puzzle lies beyond the scope of the present discussion. From what has been said, though, it is clear that in performing the duties of citizenship, we are not only contributing to the collective task of making democracy work; we also are helping to determine how power will be exercised over our fellow citizens. We are helping to determine how the democratic state will coerce *our equals.*

This is enough to suggest that the office of democratic citizenship involves a moral dimension beyond the requirement to avoid free-riding on others' political labor. We are duty-bound to contribute our fair share in maintaining democracy, but we thereby participate in an arrangement that forces our equals to comply with policies that they may oppose. To be clear, exercising power over one's subordinates raises moral questions that are familiar to anyone who raises children or supervises employees. But these are of a different kind from the questions provoked by democracy, where power is exercised over our equals. We should conclude that the role of citizen is not to be taken lightly. It is a *moral office*.

This enables us to see an additional way in which citizens must recognize one another's equality. They must dispatch the duties of citizenship with a sufficient acknowledgment that those activities carry a certain *gravity* because they involve the exercise of coercive power over their political equals. In other words, citizens must bring to their duties a certain moral sensibility. Citizens must embody what I call the *virtues* of citizenship.

Before exploring these virtues, another comment is in order about the narrow scope of the argument. Democratic theorists are fond of devising ambitious theories of "civic virtue," the traits that render a citizen an exemplary contributor to democracy's thriving. A complete theory of democracy certainly needs an account of what makes for excellent citizenship. My purposes are more modest. I am not concerned to provide an account of exemplary citizenship, but only to provide an account of what it takes for citizens to treat one another as political equals. The broader category of civic virtue is not in play. My task rather is to identify the *virtues of citizenship*, by which I mean only the traits that citizens must manifest if they are going to wield their political power in a way that duly acknowledges the equality of their fellow citizens. Three such virtues are central.

First, there is the virtue of *public-mindedness*. This is the disposition to perform the duties of citizenship in a way that manifests a concern for the *common good*, rather than strictly for narrowly conceived interests. It can be added that public-mindedness also involves the closely related disposition to seek justice and oppose injustice in political matters, even when one's own particular interests might recommend otherwise. The public-minded citizen recognizes that in performing the duties of citizenship, she is playing a part in directing the state to exert power in ways that impact *all* citizens; hence she endeavors to bring to her political activity an enlarged perspective.[4]

Second is the virtue of *reciprocity*. As their views about how power should be exercised are to be informed by consideration of the common good and justice, citizens need to formulate their political opinions *in light of* the perspectives, values, and concerns of their fellow citizens. This means that democratic citizenship calls for a willingness to engage in a reciprocal exchange of political ideas, a disposition to weigh competing considerations, a tendency to be open to objections and challenges to the views we favor, and a readiness to revise our views in light of others' perspectives. We acknowledge our fellow citizens' political equality by trying to formulate our political opinions in a way that acknowledges that our views must be the product of a give-and-take of ideas among our fellow citizens. The virtue of reciprocity is the disposition to formulate one's political views in a way that reflects a willingness not merely to allow others to speak, but to give them a hearing. We manifest the virtue of reciprocity when the views and concerns of others contribute to our own thinking.

The third virtue of citizenship is *transparency*. When deciding how to instruct the democratic state to deploy its power, citizens must not only think in terms of the common good and justice in a way that reflects a due consideration of the views of others; they must also seek to formulate their political opinions in terms that other citizens can recognize as intelligible, even if not altogether convincing or decisive. That is, citizens must endeavor to craft their political views in ways that refer to values that are commonly shared among democratic citizens. If one's political ideas are going to be the upshot of a reciprocal exchange of ideas, parties to the discussion must try to offer reasons that the others can recognize as such. This kind of transparency is required if, when citizens find that they favor opposing views, they can see one another as engaged in a *disagreement* over the common good rather than simply a conflict.

These three virtues exhibit a certain unity. We must be transparent in order to manifest the virtue of reciprocity, and reciprocity is necessary for realizing the virtue of public-mindedness. Put differently, if we are going to exercise our political power in a way that is public-minded, we need to exchange political perspectives with our fellow citizens, and such exchanges themselves must aspire to proceed from common ground. Thus, a failure to manifest any one of these three virtues generally will result in a failure to manifest the other two. Given this relation, the three virtues of citizenship are jointly necessary for duly recognizing political equality. Moving forward, it will be less cumbersome if we capture them together with a single term: *civility*.

The virtue of civility is composed of the dispositions to be public-minded, reciprocating, and transparent. We can say, then, that in order to duly recognize the political equality of one's fellow citizens, one must perform the duties of citizenship in a way that manifests the virtue of civility. More simply, citizens are required to be civil to one another when fulfilling the duties of citizenship. In the absence of civility, democratic politics becomes simply a matter of directing and deploying power, and the idea of self-government among equals is lost.

Though it is handy, the term "civility" presents difficulties. It is sometimes used to denote a calm or concessive demeanor, a disposition to avoid conflict or seek consilience for its own sake. Civility in this popular sense requires deescalation, courtesy, and conciliation in the face of disagreement. According to some views of this kind, it also requires that one manifest positive affect or a sense of community toward those with whom one disagrees.

This is not the sense of the term that I intend. Although civility in the popular sense might be admirable in some general way, it is not a virtue of citizenship—it is not a requirement for manifesting a due regard for the equality of others. This is because self-government among equals involves disagreements over some of the most important things, such as justice, freedom, autonomy, dignity, and the like. Democracy is often an uneasy enterprise. Heated tones and antagonistic demeanors are to be expected when citizens are taking democracy seriously.

Accordingly, by *civility* I mean the combined profile of the three virtues of citizenship: public-mindedness, reciprocity, and transparency. Civility in this sense involves no imperative to avoid conflict or seek appeasement. Civility is consistent with hostility and rancor; one need not *like* others in order to duly recognize their equality. Congeniality and fondness are not necessary for civility. All that civility requires is that citizens do not lose sight of the fact that their fellow citizens are their political equals, who are therefore *entitled* to an equal say. Civility in this sense is consistent with political antagonism, even some degree of enmity.

## 2.3.  Fitting the Pieces Together

I have been arguing that the democratic moral idea of political equality gives rise to a corresponding ethos composed of both duties and virtues. I recognize that the discussion has covered a lot of ground quickly. So let's take a moment to fit the pieces together.

Begin from the basics. In a democracy, citizens are political equals in the view of their government. Yet they are also one another's equals. They must treat one another accordingly. One way in which citizens treat one another as equals is by contributing their fair share to the collective task of maintaining democracy. There thus are duties of citizenship, requirements to perform the various civic tasks necessary to make democratic government work. To fail to perform these tasks is to free-ride on the political labor of others. This is to treat one's fellow citizens as less than equal.

However, making democracy work involves more than maintaining its institutions and participating in the processes that produce political decisions. These activities almost always involve directing the coercive power of the state. This poses a puzzle: in a democracy, political power is power exerted among equals. More precisely, it is power exercised *over* one's equals. The duties of citizenship thus must be dispatched in a way that reflects the moral gravity of that fact. I have argued that in order for the coercive power of the state to be exercised in a way that is consistent with the political equality of those over whom it is deployed, citizens must manifest the virtue of civility.

The overriding idea driving this account of civility is that if the exertion of power by the state is to be compatible with the political equality of its citizens, power must never be simply *inflicted* on them. To be clear, political power is always exerted over someone, and to that extent, whenever it is exercised, it is imposed. But in a democracy such power must never be *brute*. Those who wield power nonetheless must be accountable to those over whom it is deployed. In a democracy, the citizens collectively wield this power. Civility ensures that their political power remains accountable.

Here's how. When democratic citizens are subjected to political decisions and policies they do not support, they must comply, but they are never under a requirement *simply* to submit. Even when power has been directed by properly democratic processes, citizens are permitted to challenge, contest, protest, and resist. Civility is the collection of dispositions citizens must embody if those activities are going to have sufficient political *uptake* to serve their democratic function of ensuring that no citizen is ever a mere *target* of the state's power or an *object* over which force is exerted. When citizens manifest the virtue of civility, even those who most feel the imposition of political power nonetheless remain participants in self-government.

Civility thus renders the political power of the democratic state more than brute. When citizens manifest the virtue of civility, those over whom political power is exercised retain their status as political equals. Accordingly, cultivating the virtue of civility is a component of democracy's ethos.

Such is the argument from the democratic idea of political equality to the democratic ethos. It can be encapsulated succinctly: democratic citizens share power as equals, and because exercising power over one's equals is a morally weighty enterprise, there are moral requirements, in the form of duties and virtues, that attach to the role of citizen. This result is admittedly modest. For one thing, it identifies a condition for *adequate* citizenship, not a model for exemplary citizenship. Note also that it invokes no broader claims about what makes for a *good* or *competent* democratic government. Although the hope is that embodying democracy's ethos will tend to improve the quality of a citizen's political judgment, and therefore contribute to the overall soundness of government, there is no guarantee that it will have this effect. That is to say, a citizen can realize the democratic ethos and yet still have poor political judgment.

Recall that the public-mindedness component of civility is the disposition to *consider* the common good and to *seek* justice; it does not call for accurate judgments with respect to these things. Accordingly, a citizen can satisfy the demands for recognizing the political equality of her fellow citizens and nonetheless hold flawed political opinions. Therefore, a democracy in which all citizens embody the democratic ethos and thus duly respect one another's equality can nonetheless fall short of being a good society. Even when properly enacted, democracy can leave a lot to be desired. It often does.

Though it might seem dispiriting, this result is as it should be. It serves to remind us that our political foes might not be failing as citizens, that not every political disagreement is due to the opposition having given up on democracy. Moreover, it makes available to us the idea that various forms of political critique, contestation, and objection are part of the democratic ethos, rather than activities launched only in the face of democratic breakdown. In other words, the democratic ethos embeds the idea that citizens may challenge democratic laws and policies without having to claim that democracy has broken down. The argument helps us to see that the products of democratic processes are not beyond reproach.

Taken together, these considerations point to a crucial upshot. It's often observed that democracy takes a lot of work. But we now can see that democracy might be even more demanding than we realize. Even under favorable conditions, where each citizen is acting as they should, democracy will provoke ongoing disagreements, disputes, challenges, and protests among citizens. Democracy requires us to acknowledge that our opponents are nonetheless our political equals, and thus entitled to an equal say and also a hearing. That's easier said than done. To foreshadow the argument to come, democracy's ethos is difficult to sustain.

## 3. Democracy as a Practical Ideal

So far, I have been focusing on how democracy looks *in theory*. And even though I just indicated that democracy is never easy, the overall picture of democracy is still flattering. Democracy, we have seen, comes to more than the rule of the people. It is a self-governing society of dutiful and virtuous equals. Democracy is a dignifying proposal.

But there's the catch. In focusing on the theoretical implications of democracy's idea of political equality, I have not described any existing democratic society. I have developed a picture of what democracy *ought to be*, a view of democracy as an *ideal*. I have said, in effect, that democracy is the *ideal* of a self-governing society of dutiful and virtuous equals. Yet when understood as an ideal, democracy carries the seed of discontent. Put bluntly, the democratic ideal makes the real world of democracy look disastrous.

No existing society satisfies the democratic ideal. As we all know, real democracies are noisy, disorderly, frustrating, typically irrational, and reliably inefficient. Democratic politicians pander, surrogates spin, opponents obstruct, and citizens' power is largely constrained to the role of the spectator cheering (or booing) from the stands. Far from dutifully and virtuously contributing to the processes that direct political power, citizens tend to pick political sides much in the way that they might attach themselves to sports teams. When it comes to wielding power, citizens and officials alike typically act as if the whole point is to subdue the opposition. As a result, democracy operates more like a ruthless struggle for power among elites than a shared project of self-government among equal citizens. As democracy's critics have long observed, no matter what democracy may be in theory, in practice it's all spectacle.

No society satisfies the democratic ideal. But that's not the worst of it. No existing democracy will *ever* fulfill the ideal of being a self-governing society of equals. Democracies are, after all, political associations among *humans*, and we are irremediably flawed creatures. Even if we suppose, as is highly unlikely, that political corruption and ordinary dishonesty could be completely extinguished from society, there will always be citizens who do not live up to the ethos of democracy. As a result, existing societies are destined to fall short.

These considerations prompt an obvious challenge. Given the inevitability of our failure to fulfill the democratic ideal, why should anyone bother *trying* to live up to it? The duties of citizenship are not easily satisfied, and the virtues of citizenship are difficult to cultivate. What's the point?

In addressing this challenge, we need to be clear about the sense in which we have been describing an *ideal*. Imagine a physician who devotes his days to building a theoretical model of perfect health, a conception of a human body that never succumbs to illness or dysfunction of any kind. We would be right to question the utility of his endeavor, especially with respect to his business, which we can assume is healing ailing bodies. His model of flawless health probably offers no assistance in treating a sick patient. We might say that his model of the perfectly healthy body is an ideal, but one that provides no practical guidance. It is, in this sense, an impractical ideal.

Contrast this physician with a personal trainer who begins from an inventory of her client's health goals and an assessment of the client's current physical condition. She uses this information to construct an exercise and nutrition regimen, which serves as a guide to helping her client pursue the stated goals. This guide is importantly different from the physician's model in that it constructs a strategy for furthering a project. Again, by looking to the client's goals and physical condition, the trainer can evaluate progress, identify shortcomings, and even modify the plan. Her ideal can direct practice; it is in that sense a *practical ideal*.

The democratic ideal is a practical ideal. Beginning with a fundamental moral commitment to the political equality of the citizens, I then constructed a partial plan for pursuing the fulfillment of that commitment. To be sure, just as physical health is a goal that is never *achieved* in any final sense so much as *worked for* and *maintained*, democracy is an ongoing project of realizing a political order of self-governing equals. In devising an ideal of democracy, I have not set out a model, but instead identified a project, something to strive for.

Practical ideals are ideals, but they are not idle. They have teeth. Look again at the unflattering depiction of real-world democracy that was offered earlier. It was presented as a *critique* of the current state of democratic politics, or at least as something to lament. It is by appeal to the democratic ideal that we are able to recognize real-world democracies as falling short. In other words, part of what makes existing democracy frustrating and disappointing is that it misses the mark of self-government among equals in obvious ways. And our ideal helps to diagnose some of the shortcomings: citizens and officials who do not embody the virtue of civility and for that reason do not adequately recognize political equality.

The ideal of democracy is potent. It provides a basis for social critique, a stance that can assess the current state of democratic politics by pointing to the fundamental democratic commitment to political equality. In this way, the ideal supplies a perspective that is *within* democracy and yet can evaluate it. It supplies a critical stance that is *internal* to democracy.

This stance is essential. It permits citizens to distinguish between political criticism and what might be called *campaigning*. When engaged in campaigning, citizens attempt simply to sway opinion in favor of their preferred policies. To that extent, campaigners seek a definite result. The kind of political criticism enabled by the democratic ideal is different. It calls us to the fundamental values of democracy so that we might attend to the ways in which our politics is falling short of our own shared commitments. Political criticism in this sense is hence not a matter of campaigning for a change of policy *within* a democratic system; it is rather a way of exposing the respects in which the existing political arrangement is imperfectly democratic. And that kind of criticism must be rooted in ideas and principles that lie beyond our everyday political disputes. That style of criticism instead proceeds from the shared vision within which ordinary politics is conducted. The democratic ideal makes that shared vision explicit and thus available for deployment in efforts to more completely realize democracy.

Democracy is therefore a *social aspiration* rather than a form of government or a system of politics. It is the *aspiration* for a society of self-governing political equals. Does that mean that no existing society counts as democratic? Not exactly.

Yes, every existing society falls short of being a self-governing society of political equals. However, we should classify some existing societies as democracies because of what they aspire to be. To be clear, just as someone who never exercises and eats only candy can hardly be said to aspire to physical health, there are institutional conditions a society must meet if it is to count as democratic. These include a stable infrastructure of accountable and representative government, regular open elections, an independent judiciary, a free press, legal protections for dissenters, an orientation toward the rule of law, and so on.

These are among the materially necessary conditions that must be met if an existing society is to count as democratic. Yet they are not sufficient. The society must also embrace the aspiration of more completely fulfilling the idea of political equality. In order to do this, the society must recognize the force of the practical ideal of democracy; it must recognize itself as incompletely democratic. This means that it must stand vulnerable to the political criticism of its citizens and seek to progress in the direction of a fuller realization of the ideal. Therefore, no matter how things stand with respect to its institutions, when a society gives up the pursuit of more completely realizing the democratic ideal, it begins to fail as a democracy.

## 4. The Generality of the Account

This chapter has set out a view of democracy as the practical ideal of a self-governing society of equals. I hope this view will be acceptable to readers across a broad range of political perspectives. In other words, I have sought to propose a view of democracy that is itself nonpartisan. Even though I expect liberals, conservatives, progressives, and libertarians will disagree over the details of my view, I also take it that these camps will not disagree deeply about the idea of political equality, or even the duties and virtues I have discussed.

It is important that my conception of democracy be nonpartisan in this way. This is because the central problem this book addresses is intended to be general: my contention is that the democrat's dilemma plagues democratic citizens *as such*. If this is correct, then any characterization of democracy that fully evades the dilemma will also involve an abandoning of some central element of democracy itself.

In any case, the rudiments have been set in place. I have laid out a conception of democracy from which we can explore the democrat's dilemma and the corresponding challenge of sustaining democracy.

# 2

# Why Sustain Democracy?

Late in September 2001 some colleagues at my university organized a teach-in focused on President George W. Bush's plan to invade Afghanistan in response to the September 11 terrorist attacks. I have always been wary of deployments of military force, and in this case the proposed invasion struck me as especially ill-conceived. I assumed that there was some dimension of Bush's strategy that I had overlooked, some rationale for the invasion that I had not considered. I attended the teach-in hoping to learn what it could be.

The presentations at the event were uniform in content. Each speaker unequivocally condemned the looming invasion, claiming it to be illegal, inhumane, unnecessary, and counterproductive, but none addressed—or even identified—the reasons the Bush administration had given for its support. To be clear, various rationales were ascribed, but these were always framed as the *true* but *unstated* purposes driving the policy: the seizure of oil, the awarding of military contracts to campaign donors, and so on. No speaker mentioned the reasons that the supporters of the plan offered in its defense.

I found myself in agreement with much of what my colleagues were saying about the imprudence, illegality, and immorality of the invasion. Their assessments of the proposed invasion generally matched my own. But I still had no greater sense of what the proposed rationale for the invasion was. I wasn't *learning* very much at the teach-in.

The question period began with several comments that reinforced the sentiments that already had been expressed. Many comments sought to intensify the condemnation. One audience member went so far as to suggest that the administration wanted the invasion *because* it would be so lawless and cruel. Another attributed the proposed invasion to a desire on Bush's part to prompt an apocalyptic holy war between the West and the East. Still another called for the immediate arrest of President Bush, Vice President Cheney, and Secretary Donald Rumsfeld.

Eventually there was a welcome lull in the room, and the fervor seemed to ease slightly. I put my hand up and asked why none of the speakers had addressed any of the reasons that those who supported Bush's proposal offered in its defense. The main organizer seemed affronted. He responded that if I wanted to defend Bush, I was welcome to step up to do so. defensive

Stunned, I replied that in fact I also opposed the invasion and did not support the president's policy. I then added that I had come to the event hoping that someone would at least *identify* the rationale of its supporters, even if ultimately to challenge it. I further emphasized that I was not calling for "both sides" or "equal time," but only wished that some attempt be made to come to grips with what Bush's supporters offered as the best reasons for the invasion. This, I said, would be necessary to formulate a sound critique of Bush's proposal, which I had assumed was central to the objective of the teach-in.

With a tone of pity, another panelist replied that I had mistakenly assumed that Bush and his supporters "use reason," adding that such an assumption was "dangerous" because it gave them "too much credit." Another chimed in with the claim that "too much is at stake" to treat the policy as a matter for "armchair debate"; he then hollered, "It's time to *act!*" Audience members offered similar rebukes, and the discussion returned to its prior trajectory.

I was mistaken about the purpose of the teach-in. The aim was not to examine the rationale for the proposed invasion, but rather to rally around a specific evaluation of it, to join others in condemning it and possibly thereby learn new reasons for opposing it. The prevailing attitude in the room was that this kind of assembly was necessary: *The political situation is dire, and we need to take a stand. The time for weighing the various perspectives has expired. If you think there's another side to the discussion, you must be on it. And if you're on the other side, there's nothing to discuss.*

This anecdote is likely to strike familiar notes with many readers, especially those who have been involved in political organizing and activism. Yet the resulting tune is strained. On the one hand, we must act on behalf of justice as we see it. On the other, we must proceed in ways that duly recognize the equality of our fellow citizens, including those who oppose our ideas about what justice requires. Yet when we're in the throes of political action, our rivals often seem to be obstacles rather than democratic partners. Trying to understand their resistance or grasp their professed point of view seems a distraction, or worse, a diversion. Their political views seem to us so distorted that we imagine them to be incapable of engaging honestly in democracy. The requirements of democracy pull us in two different directions. Hence the democrat's dilemma.

Let's formulate the dilemma in a little more detail. The issues that provoke us to engage politically often strike us as *urgent* in a way that demands swift and decisive action. Yet in democratic politics, we almost never can work alone. If we want a political voice, we need to join a chorus. We need to collaborate with others who share our objectives; we need to organize and build coalitions with like-minded fellow citizens. These formations are effective when the members share assurances of their solidarity and commitment to the aims of the group. Often, this prompts regular expressions of disdain for viewpoints that run contrary to those of the coalition. Such expressions usually include negative assessments of those who espouse the opposing ideas, the people on the other side.

Political alliances are essential to a well-functioning democracy. However, as noted in Chapter 1, it's part of the democratic ethos to manifest civility in one's political engagements. This requires citizens to at least *attempt* to consider the ideas, concerns, and arguments of their fellow citizens, including those they regard as political foes. Yet doing so can signal to our collaborators a lack of commitment. In trying to formulate a charitable account of where the opposition stands, we risk seeming halfhearted to our allies. This in turn can weaken coalitions and undermine our political aims.

This tension within the office of citizenship occasions the democrat's dilemma. Familiar and commendable modes of political engagement press us toward attitudes and dispositions that contravene the virtue of civility and thus erode the democratic ethos. Yet those same attitudes and dispositions often are politically potent. Democracy takes endurance, after all, and citizens need to stay focused and energized.

What's more, as my colleagues at the teach-in revealed, when we are in the midst of politics, it often seems to us that the other side is, indeed, failing to be reasonable and thus failing at democracy. When we are confronting urgent political matters, it strikes us that those who oppose us are ill-motivated, corrupt, untrustworthy, and likely dangerous.[1] We see them as divested from civility and disinclined to uphold the democratic ethos.

Under these circumstances, citizens naturally ask themselves why they ought to sustain democratic relations with their political foes. More than this, it's a perfectly *valid* question, one that citizens ought to ask. It's plausible to think that when push comes to shove in democracy, civility should take a backseat to the aim of achieving the correct result. As my colleague at the teach-in observed, there are times when too much is at stake.

After all, we tend to view our political opponents as not merely on the *other* side, but on the *wrong* side, which is also the *unjust* side. One might query: Why treat advocates of injustice as equal partners in democracy? Why not disregard their perspective? Why bother trying to address their ideas? Why trust them to uphold the norms of democratic citizenship? Why not momentarily cast aside the virtue of civility and regard the other side as enemy combatants in a cold civil war? In short, when the moral stakes are high, why uphold democracy's ethos? Why should we sustain democracy?

That's the democrat's dilemma in a nutshell. Yet the nutshell version is, naturally, only a preliminary formulation. In order to capture the weight and nuance of the dilemma, I need to do a lot of unpacking. That's the task of this chapter. I will portray the dilemma as a real challenge that responsible democratic citizens confront in the course of their political engagement. In other words, I aim to present the dilemma in a way that is *sympathetic* to the possibility that my colleagues at the teach-in had the right idea.

The democrat's dilemma is complex. In order to spell it out, I will need to present a range of considerations, and then pull them together. I begin from the perspective of the democratic citizen. From there, I will expand the focus to include interactions among citizens who find themselves on opposing political sides. This will enable us to see the dilemma as emerging from the stance of the responsible democratic citizen, rather than emerging out of some kind of political negligence. I will show that our responsibilities as citizens not only *give rise* to the question of whether to sustain democracy—they *warrant* it.

## 1. Seeing the Dilemma from the Inside

To get started, it's important to cast the democrat's dilemma in the right light, to see it as more than an intellectual puzzle emanating from the theorist's armchair. We need to recognize that the tension arises from within the purview of the engaged citizen. It is activated by citizens' attempts to take seriously their role as active participants in self-government and fed by their commitment to justice. To locate firmly this *internal* source of the dilemma, let's stick with the nutshell formulation provided earlier and consider a response that it might provoke.

Perhaps the democrat's dilemma can be easily dismissed. One could argue that treating fellow citizens—including one's political adversaries—as one's equals is *itself* a requirement of justice. The argument might continue that the conflict between pursuing justice and treating rivals as equals is thus merely apparent. Sustaining democracy when we assess our political foes as favoring injustice might be a problem of marshaling the will to do so—but that's a question of *how* to bring oneself to sustain democracy, not of *why* one should. Insofar as the democrat's dilemma has to do with *why* one should sustain democracy, the answer is easy: justice demands it. The democrat's dilemma dissolves. Case closed.

This direct response is undeniably attractive. In Chapter 3, I will endorse a modified version of it. That is, in the end I will argue that our commitment to justice both occasions the democrat's dilemma and supplies its resolution. As things stand, however, the simple reply is not decisive, not even against the nutshell version of the dilemma.

To see that the simple reply does not dissolve the democrat's dilemma, notice that it treats the problem from above, or perhaps from *outside*, the perspective of the citizen. The reply depicts the dilemma as a conflict between two imperatives—*work for justice* and *treat fellow citizens as equals*—and then asserts that upholding the latter is necessary for satisfying the former. However, although the conflict between justice and equality is indeed at the core of the dilemma, the difficulty is not simply one of managing conflicting imperatives. It's not a dilemma in that strictly formal sense. It runs deeper.

To repeat, when in the throes of disputes over urgent political questions, we often *feel* pulled in opposing moral directions, caught between the clashing imperatives of seeking justice and treating others as equals. We hence are *conflicted*. The challenge of sustaining democracy has to do with the citizen's *integrity*. In order to grasp the democrat's dilemma, then, we need to look at it from the inside. We need to recognize that when the imperatives conflict, it can strike us that recognizing our opponents' equality, and engaging with them as civility demands, is itself a kind of concession to injustice—an appeasement, a rotten compromise.[2]

Here's how. Although political theorists sometimes talk about political opinions as the "preferences" and "choices" that citizens express in their political behavior, these terms are too anemic to capture how we relate to our own political ideas. Our views about politics are driven by our conception of justice. In saying that, I do not mean that citizens walk around with sophisticated philosophical theories in their heads. They don't. My claim rather is that *we take ourselves* to have more or less orderly ideas about what makes for a free and decent society and how the political world generally ought to be organized. These ideas in turn inform our opinions about which kind of political policies are best and what sorts of things government ought to do. That's how it seems to us, at any rate.

Whether in fact our political ideas hang together coherently is irrelevant. The point is that we take our views to be well organized; we see them as systematic. Accordingly, we also see our opinions about specific political issues as informed by our more general background commitments about how things ought to be. That's all I am referring to: a person's overall view of what's politically proper. In calling this a *conception of justice*, nothing loftier is implied.

It is by reference to our conception of justice that we arrive at our ideas about how to deploy our share of political power in particular cases—what causes to support, which political policies to endorse, which candidates to vote for, what political party to join (if any), and so on.[3] Thus, when it comes to the political questions we regard as momentous, our votes and other modes of advocacy do more than register our preferences. The preferences expressed in our political behavior strike us as reflections of our judgments about what's good and right, what *ought to be done*. This is why we commonly experience electoral losses as *defeats* and *setbacks* rather than as mere dissatisfactions. When it comes to the political issues that matter to us, our views invoke judgments that express our conception of justice.

Yet there is a sense in which our conception of justice also expresses us. We tend to *identify* with our political views. We *invest* in them. We define ourselves in their terms. This is why we typically describe our political views not merely as beliefs we hold, but rather as *who we are*. We say things like "I'm pro-life," "I'm a pacifist," "I'm a free-marketeer," and so on. In contexts where more general political matters are under discussion, we say things like "I'm a liberal," "I'm a progressive," "I'm a libertarian," or "I'm a conservative"; in the United States in particular, we tend to identify with our party affiliation, Republican or Democrat.

Rarely do we report our political views in the same way that we might announce our beliefs about, say, the time of day or the weather. Politics runs deeper than that. This is why we often preface statements of our political opinions about specific matters with an identification of our political allegiance: "As a conservative, I believe that . . ." Our larger political perspectives help to explain our positions in particular cases. Declaring them enables others to situate our more particular views, to see where we stand.

In short, our views concerning justice tend to reach within our sense of ourselves. They are our *commitments, stances,* or *orientations*. In this way, they function like religious affiliations.[4] They play a leading role not only in making us who we are, but also in helping us to *understand* ourselves. They are more than beliefs that we hold. In a way, they hold us.

That we identify ourselves by means of our conception of justice means that we also use it to *locate* ourselves socially. We instinctively seek friendship and community with others whom we regard as like ourselves in the relevant respects. As our commitments about justice are central to how we define ourselves, they hence also tend to establish our social identities—our sense of where we belong in the social world. Our political stance situates us within a larger social nexus that is by and large structured according to group affiliations and antipathies. It is by means of our conception of justice that we identify who our political friends and foes are, and thus get our political bearings.

Indeed, to make a point to which we will return throughout this book, in the United States and elsewhere, political allegiances and affiliations increasingly reflect entire lifestyles rather than just political opinions. We might say that our partisan political identities have become ever more *central* to our overall sense of ourselves.[5] Our occupations, parenting styles, consumer habits, and aesthetic sensibilities are tightly bound to our political identities.[6] Where we buy groceries, the neighborhood we live in, the work we do, and even how we vacation are reliable predictors of our politics. This means that our social lives are increasingly partitioned by politics into distinct spaces, physical and otherwise. As "liberal" and "conservative" have become distinct ways of life, they have also grown to be separate communities.

Now for the upshot. Given that we identify with our conception of justice, the demand to regard our fellow citizens—including our political adversaries—as our equals can give rise to something like a crisis of conscience. In recognizing our political foes as our fellow citizens, it feels as if we have *conceded* something to them. The recognition of their equality can seem like a tacit acknowledgment that opposing views might be correct or acceptable. Striving to maintain civil relations with them has the flavor of capitulation, appeasement, and surrender.

This in turn can feel like inauthenticity, a lapse of integrity, a betraying of our commitments and thus of ourselves. Furthermore, as our political commitments structure relations with others, inauthenticity can look to our allies, who are often also our friends, like *disloyalty* or *desertion*. Civility can make us look "soft" to our allies. When we treat our opponents as our equals, we thus can strain our political friendships, undo our civic bonds, and leave ourselves socially unmoored. This, in turn, weakens our chances of achieving our political aims, aims we regard as just.

This is why the simple response to the democrat's dilemma is facile. Although it may be true in the end that justice requires one to uphold one's commitment to treating opponents as one's equals, that bald assertion is not enough to dissolve the problem. In fact, it's bound to fall flat. It overlooks the *internal* aspect of the dilemma, the inner conflict of integrity that occasions it. It similarly misses the fact that the challenge of sustaining democracy emerges from *within* the situated perspective of citizens who take their political responsibilities seriously. That is, the democrat's dilemma arises out of a concern to further justice, to better realize the democratic aspiration. The issue, then, is not simply *how* we can muster the will to sustain democracy, but *why we should.*

Seeing the democrat's dilemma from the inside is only a first step toward its complete articulation. To gain further clarity, we need to approach it from a different angle. Having situated the dilemma within the perspective of the democratic citizen, we now need to see how it emerges *interpersonally*, from the ways that citizens interact when they are politically engaged.

## 2. Persistent Political Disagreement

Recall that democracy is fundamentally a commitment to political equality. A direct consequence of political equality is that citizens are entitled to make up their own minds about politics. As we are equal partners in self-government, we are each at liberty to exercise our own judgment in deciding how we will exercise our share of political power. Because we are equals, no citizen is owed another's *deference* or *agreement* in political matters. For better or worse, we are free to form our own opinions, using whatever methods we judge appropriate.

Of course, even though no one is owed our deference, we frequently defer to others when forming our political views. We seek to toe the party line or stand in unity with our allies, and this leads us to align our judgments with theirs. Moreover, it's often *rational* to defer to others, especially when they have relevant knowledge or expertise that we lack. Although no one gets to tell us what we must think about politics, there certainly are people who *know better* than we do about political matters. Thus, there are instances in which it is imprudent, and perhaps negligent, not to defer to the political judgment of another citizen. Nevertheless, garden varieties of political irrationality, foolishness, pigheadedness, and carelessness are not criminal, even though they are almost always blameworthy or at the very least lamentable.

Everyone has a right to their own opinion. This holds even when weighty reasons show the opinion in question to be false, unfounded, or implausible. This right derives from our political equality. Accordingly, even though having sound political judgment is something we ought to aspire to, it is not strictly a requirement for democratic citizenship. One wonders how it could be. Who would get to decide what sound political judgment amounts to? What would count as an adequate measure of a person's political wisdom? The most a democratic society can do is attempt to foster adequate political judgment in its citizens. Several common democratic institutions, from public education and library systems to the free press, aim in part at serving this function.

In any case, as political equality entails that citizens are entitled to exercise their own judgment about politics, democracies are awash in differences of political opinion. The democratic environment thus is populated by various groups—parties, organizations, associations, action committees, foundations, and so on—that promote specific political causes and policies. Typically, for each such group, there are several opposing groups that press for alternative platforms. These various federations vie for citizens' support and allegiance. The result is that citizens take up their various political stances, and in the course of ordinary political interaction, they discover that they disagree with one another.

Political disagreements are notorious for being unpleasant. You probably are familiar with the bit of folk wisdom recommending that one should never discuss politics over the dinner table. I suppose you also recognize that generally this is judicious counsel. Political wrangling can strain social relations in ways that ruin more than meals. I suspect you know of a friendship or familial bond that has been spoiled by political differences. Still, even though it is advisable to avoid political disputation in certain social contexts, democracy requires that we *at some point* express and engage our political differences. What's more, the intensity with which we conduct our political debates is understandable, given that politics is generally of great import. To recall a point from Chapter 1, democratic politics is largely a matter of deciding how power ought to be exercised over our political equals. That's morally serious business.

Despite the heat and vehemence that typically characterize political disagreement, we must not lose sight of the fact that in a democracy, such disputes remain interactions among equals. In other words, democracy requires citizens to recognize that at least some of their political adversaries are not disqualified from citizenship simply because they are our adversaries, and that even when engaged in bitter political debate, interlocutors must regard one another as political equals.

We all realize that this is easier said than done. Accordingly, we need to develop a conception of what might be called *good-faith* political disagreement, disagreement that may be focused on monumental political issues, but nonetheless can be engaged among conscientious and competent citizens.

## 2.1.  Good-Faith Political Disagreement

A good deal of political disagreement in a democratic society can be attributed to stubbornness, negligence, or even depravity. Various forms of political ignorance and irrationality are rampant among the citizenry of most contemporary democracies. As Winston Churchill is said to have once observed, the best argument against democracy is a five-minute conversation with the average voter. Furthermore, when we're in the midst of an animated dispute about an important political issue, the ignorance or stupidity of our interlocutor often is our preferred explanation of the fact that they disagree. In such circumstances, it seems to us that our opponents are being thick, disingenuous, or obstinate. We chalk disagreement up to the cognitive and moral flaws of our detractors. Note, however, that we almost never apply this diagnosis to our allies. Political ignorance, irrationality, and pigheadedness are always the other side's flaws.

It is comforting, in a way, to think that our political opinions are so obviously correct that no right-thinking person could possibly reject them. There's a political benefit to thinking this way, too. When we explain political disagreement by attributing obtuseness to our opposition, we thereby deny, at least implicitly, that they can pose legitimate challenges to our view. We more readily regard them as incapable of civility, and thus as obstacles to be surmounted rather than as partners in democracy who must be engaged as our equals. As we will discuss in Chapter 3, painting the opposition as a mere impediment is a reliable way to provoke political action among one's allies. Calling attention to the depravity of the other side serves as an effective way to rally our troops. It's good strategy.

Stepping back from the political fray, though, we realize that the world just is not that simple. Despite how things may appear when we're in the thick of politics, not all disagreement is due to our opponents' shortcomings. What's more, our own political views are not nearly so manifestly true as we like to think. In forming our political opinions, we all confront various limitations. None of us has perfect command of all the relevant facts, and our political judgment can always be improved. More often than we like to admit, we learn from our foes, too. And we can learn from them even when their opinions are flawed. That they're mistaken about politics doesn't entail that they can't pose hard questions and raise difficult challenges to our views.

In other words, when we're reflecting honestly, we recognize that it is possible for conscientious and competent citizens to disagree, even about monumental political questions. We can say that such disagreement is in *good faith*. In recognizing the possibility of good-faith political disagreement, we acknowledge that our political differences are not simply the *upshot* of our entitlement to make up our own minds about politics. They often are the *product* of our attempts to think deeply and responsibly about politics. Sometimes we disagree *despite* our sincerity, goodwill, and competence.

Good-faith political disagreement is possible because important political questions tend to be messy. They invoke mixtures of complex empirical, normative, and practical considerations that are often difficult to organize. That is, in thinking through the political issues that divide us, we are immediately confronted with a range of more complicated questions. These complexities create room for sincere and competent people to draw diverging conclusions, even when they are looking at the same basic facts, so to speak.

To get a clearer sense of this, consider the question of whether the state should adopt the death penalty. Even though people tend to be quick in affirming a stance on the issue, it invokes a range of tricky questions. Some of these include empirical questions such as whether the death penalty deters crime or provides psychological closure to victims. Other questions are strictly normative: Does any offender *deserve* to be executed? Is capital punishment ever *just*? Add to these an assortment of practical issues regarding capital punishment as policy: How should the state fund executions? Are reliable execution methods available? What steps can the state take in order to ensure that the death penalty would be fairly imposed?

Experts in the relevant fields disagree about all of these matters. Moreover, arriving at a verdict on whether the state should adopt capital punishment involves more than finding reliable answers to the more complicated questions the issue invokes. One's position on the death penalty implicitly prioritizes the different considerations I have mentioned, along with many others. For example, some hold that the death penalty is inconsistent with justice, and so must be opposed regardless of whether it deters crime or provides closure. Others hold that although the death penalty is justified in principle, there's no way for the state to guarantee its fair application in practice, and so it must be rejected. Still others hold that the issue turns exclusively on whether capital punishment deters crime.

Each of these positions offers its own way of weighing up the various questions the policy invokes. And a good deal of disagreement over the death penalty, even among the experts, arises from these different ways of *framing* the issue. This naturally introduces further complexities. The question of how to frame the issue of capital punishment is even messier than the empirical, normative, and practical questions just mentioned. It's no wonder, then, that sincere and competent citizens can come to diverging conclusions.

This is an overly simplified example, of course. That's deliberate, as the more realistic cases are messier still. We should conclude, then, that good-faith political disagreement is not only *possible* among citizens; it is also to be *expected*. Actually, we should say something stronger. Political disagreement is bound to *persist* even among democratic citizens who are earnestly and intelligently thinking about the issues they face. Not only will such citizens disagree over politics, but it's unlikely that their disagreements will resolve anytime soon. This means, additionally, that stable and enduring political unanimity should be viewed with suspicion. We should regard widespread uniformity of political opinion as evidence that opposing ideas and critical voices are being suppressed.

The "loyal opposition" is indispensable to a well-functioning democracy. We could say further that ongoing good-faith disputation among adamant proponents of conflicting ideas is a positive indication of democracy's health. Not only is it a consequence of political equality, it's also the product of citizens' taking their responsibilities seriously. More than this, when engaging in good-faith political disagreements, citizens recognize one another's partnership in the shared task of democracy. The activity of disagreeing in good-faith *expresses* our recognition of the political equality of our interlocutors. Were they not our equals, why would we bother exchanging ideas with them?

## 2.2. Limits to Good-Faith Political Disagreement

Not all political disagreement is in good faith. There are limits to civility's demands. Some political views are simply *beyond the pale* in a democracy. Such views are incompatible with the fundamental democratic commitment to self-government among political equals. They typically advocate some form of political hierarchy of subordinates and superiors, call for political arrangements that would deny to some citizens the entitlement to participate as political equals, and seek on that basis to expel or block some from the office of citizenship. Familiar forms of racism, sexism, and nationalism are among the views that obviously fit this mold. To keep things tidy, we can repurpose a term that John Rawls introduced to characterize political ideas that run contrary to democratic fundamentals. He called such political views, along with the people who espouse them, *unreasonable*.[7]

As they deny that all citizens are their equals, there's no good-faith disagreement to be had with proponents of unreasonable views. Unreasonable citizens therefore need not be afforded the kind of consideration that civility otherwise requires. Proper democratic citizens need not uphold democratic relations with unreasonable citizens, even though in some cases the unreasonable may retain an equal share of political power. Although as a practical matter it might be advisable under certain conditions to try to engage with unreasonable citizens *as if* they were reasonable, they nonetheless are not *deserving* of civility. In most cases, adopting unreasonable political views would be enough to render one *unfit* for democratic citizenship, regardless of whether one retains the legal status of citizen.

At the very least, we can say that citizens who embrace unreasonable political views are always proper targets of disapproval, criticism, and rebuke. Depending on the political influence a specific unreasonable doctrine has, one is permitted to regard unreasonable citizens as political obstacles to be surmounted rather than partners to be engaged. Beyond this, the question of what, precisely, reasonable citizens should do about those who are unreasonable depends on the specific details of actual cases.

Larger questions loom about how a democratic *government* should deal with unreasonable citizens. Again, this depends on the facts in specific instances, including details regarding the kind of political behavior the unreasonable citizens in question are engaged in. At the limits, one could imagine political views that are so radically opposed to political equality that living according to their dictates would be criminal. In other kinds of cases, one could imagine the state adopting a policy of begrudging tolerance. In order to speak beyond generalities of this kind, we would need to look at specific cases. Our concern lies elsewhere.

To be specific, we are concerned to identify the *features* that a political view must have if it is to count as beyond the pale. I have suggested that a political view is unreasonable if it is incompatible with the commitment to a society of self-governing political equals. A citizen counts as unreasonable insofar as he espouses such a view. Democratic citizens are not required to sustain democratic relations with the unreasonable.

This account will dissatisfy some readers. Apart from the obviously unreasonable doctrines I mentioned earlier, the account doesn't enable us to draw up a list of unreasonable political ideas. The proposed conception of unreasonableness captures easy cases—Nazis and the like—but doesn't offer much in the hard cases. For example, one is left to wonder whether religious doctrines that embrace a strictly patriarchal view of marriage are therefore unreasonable. Do cultural practices that assign traditional gender roles to children run counter to political equality? Are adherents of those practices unreasonable? Does legal abortion deny the equality of citizens? Are policies that permanently strip felons of their voting power unreasonable? Additional examples can be catalogued easily.

It is true that the account on offer does not deliver verdicts in these cases, at least not instantaneously. However, this kind of indeterminacy is unavoidable unless we delve into the details of specific examples. But the task is not to draw up a list of unreasonable views, only to set forth an intuitive view about what makes a view unreasonable. Although this account leaves questions about specific views unanswered, it promotes a determinate view about what we are saying when we claim that a view is beyond the pale. In calling a political view unreasonable, we are not indicating only that it conflicts with our own sense of what justice requires; we are also saying that it is incompatible with the very idea of democracy as a self-governing society of political equals. This is important because it allows us to formulate the crucial thought that there are political ideas that are inconsistent with justice but not unreasonable.

Let's regroup. While acknowledging that there are limits to what democratic citizens must recognize as worthy of civil engagement, I have argued that ongoing political disagreement is the inevitable upshot of political equality, even when citizens are responsible and sincere. In this sense, persistent good-faith political disagreement is a sign of democracy's health. But that's a political theorist's way of talking. When considered from the perspective of the citizen, we see the challenge lurking beneath the platitudes.

To make the next point, I need to borrow again from Rawls. Just as he used the term *unreasonable* to characterize proponents of political views that are beyond the pale in a democratic society, he also spoke of *reasonable* views and citizens. We can treat *reasonable* as simply the antonym of *unreasonable*. Reasonable views are compatible with the fundamental democratic commitment to a society of self-governing political equals. Reasonable citizens affirm reasonable views.

In calling a citizen reasonable, we are not thereby claiming that she is adequately dutiful or virtuous. A citizen is reasonable strictly in virtue of holding a reasonable political view. A reasonable citizen can therefore still fail to meet the standards of duty and virtue associated with decent citizenship; a reasonable citizen can be inadequately civil. Reasonableness is a low bar.

Moreover, in calling a political view reasonable, we are attributing to it no merit beyond its compatibility with democratic fundamentals.[8] Reasonableness is therefore distinct from truth and plausibility. To see how, imagine a view according to which humans are the creation of extraterrestrial amphibians that imbued us all with equal shares of a special substance that renders us political equals in charge of our own collective destiny. This view is compatible with the idea of a self-governing society of equals. It is therefore reasonable. Political views can be reasonable even though they are false. There also are implausible but nonetheless reasonable political ideas. So there are reasonable political views that contradict other reasonable political views. Most importantly, there are reasonable political views that contradict our own views.

We naturally take our own political ideas to be true or in some other sense correct. Therefore, as democratic citizens, we are required to recognize that some competing political views are reasonable, even though we assess them as also wrong, implausible, or otherwise flawed. This entails that we are also required to acknowledge that some of our political opponents are reasonable, despite the fact that we assess them as endorsing political views that are wrong. Acknowledging this much is, after all, necessary if one is to allow the possibility of good-faith political disagreement.

Now comes the hard part. Political disagreements among reasonable citizens are real *disagreements*, exchanges where each party assesses the other as in error. And, given that they're *political* disagreements, they can be animated, volatile, frustrating, and bitter. Nothing in the foregoing account has suggested that good-faith disagreements must be placid or mannerly. Recognizing a view as reasonable does not commit us to seeing it as acceptable or in the least bit agreeable. Similarly, recognizing a fellow citizen as reasonable does not preclude us from regarding her views as deserving of vehement criticism and unequivocal reproach. Reasonable citizens must recognize one another as political equals, and thus as full partners in democracy. But they need not *like* one another or see one another as allies or collaborators. Consequently, good-faith disagreements may be adversarial and even nasty. They often are.

Recall that we regard our political views as more than merely our *preferences*. As was argued earlier, they are tied to our broader commitments about how things *ought to be*, politically speaking. They reflect our conception of justice and are in that sense normative. Consequently, when engaging the political issues that most concern us, we are bound to regard our opposition's views as not simply undesirable or less choiceworthy than our own. Rather, we must see them as *wrong*. And in this context, "wrong" must mean something like *missing the mark* of justice, *incompatible* with justice, or perhaps flatly *unjust*. In addition, we must adopt the attitude that, were the opposition's ideas to prevail politically, the result would count as a *setback* or maybe an *affront* to justice. We therefore are bound to regard at least some of our political opponents as advocates of injustice, at least to some degree.[9] This accounts for why even good-faith political disagreements are so often unpleasant.

## 2.3. The Dilemma Restated

I can now add additional detail to the democrat's dilemma. We are bound to assess even our reasonable political opponents as favoring policies and platforms that are mistaken about politics, and therefore to some degree not just. We readily acknowledge the possibility and value of good-faith political disagreement *in principle*; however, when embroiled in real-world politics, we far more commonly explain our disagreements by pointing to the opposition's defects and failures. It seems to us that those on the other side have neglected to think clearly about the issues in a way that takes into full account all of the relevant factors, including the perspectives and concerns of their fellow citizens. They seem to us to be shortsighted, self-centered, misinformed, benighted, or even depraved. It also strikes us that these flaws *explain* why they hold such degenerate opinions. In other words, we tend to diagnose our opponents as either failing at civility or, at worst, not even interested in it.

It often seems to us that even though our opponents might espouse *views* that are reasonable, they are too lost or corrupt to be invested in democracy. They of course may give lip service to the value of good-faith political disagreement among conscientious citizens, but it strikes us that in doing this they're actually running a con. Their appeals to the democratic ethos serve merely to hold us to the requirements of citizenship so that they can more easily free-ride on our good civic behavior. So we tend to regard our opponents as acting in democratic bad faith. Accordingly, our political disagreements with them cannot be in good faith.

Under such conditions, it strikes us as naive to sustain democracy. It may also appear *unjust* to do so. Upholding our democratic commitments when dealing with unscrupulous and uncivil opponents cedes to them a political advantage: we play by the rules of democracy, but they don't. Given that it is *also* part of the democratic ethos to exercise our political power in ways that help to further justice, responsible citizens hence confront the democrat's dilemma. They uphold civility at the expense of optimizing the chances of achieving political outcomes that they regard as just. Consequently, when the political stakes are high, it seems that we ought to suspend democracy. Rather than trying to maintain civil relations with our foes, we should drop the façade of democracy's ethos and go to battle for the sake of justice.

When pursuing justice, why shouldn't we suspend democracy? To appreciate the full force of this question, note that in confronting the democrat's dilemma, citizens need not go so far as to advocate for a *wholesale* rejection of the democratic principle of political equality. That would render them unreasonable. Nor are we considering instances where citizens seek to deploy violence or other extralegal measures against their political rivals. We are not considering cases where citizens might try to forcibly suppress, disenfranchise, punish, or imprison their political foes. There are political conditions that would justify citizens in taking extreme measures in defense of democracy. But the democrat's dilemma is more subtle.

When in the grip of the democrat's dilemma, citizens are considering a *temporary* suspension of the democratic ethos for the limited purposes of securing a just policy outcome. They are asking why they should uphold the virtue of civility in dealing with their adversaries, given the political stakes. Instead of engaging in reciprocal and transparent interactions aimed at discerning a common good, why not seek to shut down the opposition? Why not regard them, at least for the time being, as people who may get an equal say, but are too impaired or depraved to be really *deserving* of one? When it comes to momentous political decisions, it often seems warranted to set aside the virtue of civility and just engage in a kind of realpolitik that respects the legal or formal equality of the other side but nonetheless attempts to disrupt and dominate them so that justice might prevail.

## 3. The Burden of Citizenship

Let's pull the threads together. I began by observing that the democrat's dilemma emerges within the perspective of the reasonable and conscientious citizen. Insofar as we are citizens of this kind, we take seriously our responsibility to contribute our fair share to the common tasks of democracy in ways that manifest a due regard for the political equality of our fellow citizens. We thus seek to formulate our political ideas in ways that take due consideration of the perspectives, concerns, and ideas of our fellow citizens. We strive to be civil. But we also recognize the duty to act on behalf of justice as we understand it.

Because our political advocacy expresses our commitments about justice, we are bound to regard our political adversaries as not merely incorrect or misinformed about politics, but politically *misguided*. We must see those on the other side as not only wrong, but also *in the wrong*. And when it comes to political issues that strike us as momentous, to be on the side that's wrong is also to be on the side of injustice. Democratic citizenship, then, requires that we recognize some citizens as our equals, even though we also regard them as advocating injustice. Insofar as they are reasonable, we must strive to maintain civil relations with them, even though we also regard them as bitter political foes.

And there's more. According to the democratic ethos, we must also judge it *right* that our reasonable opponents have an equal political say, even though we assess their views as incompatible with justice. And when they prevail politically, we must regard it as legitimate for democratic government to enact their will. Proper citizens thus must commit to the idea that there is a range of unjust political policies whose endorsement is consistent with proper citizenship and whose enactment is consistent with legitimate government. Sustaining democracy is a matter of upholding these commitments even in the midst of intense political engagement over matters that strike us as urgent and momentous. That's asking a lot.

Yet democracy is more demanding still. Our views about justice serve as *commitments* with which we identify, stances that help us define ourselves. Our political commitments also situate us in various social relations of allyship and opposition with others. Our social identities hence are fixed largely by our conception of justice.

Remember an earlier point: our political commitments have *depth* within our self-understanding and group identity.

Thus, democratic citizenship involves an oddly conflicted moral posture. Given the depth of our political commitments, the requirement to regard our opponents as our equals can feel alienating. Our foes seek to create a political world that we are bound to assess as less than just. Furthermore, we tend to explain our opposition's unjust political views as the result of their disingenuous commitment to the democratic ethos. In treating them civilly, we seem to be offering them *assistance*. This feels like capitulation, infidelity to our principles.

Add to this that our political commitments typically draw us into collaborations with like-minded others in pursuit of shared political objectives. If we want to achieve political results, we often need to build or join a coalition. These formations thrive when members are assured of one another's authentic commitment to the group's goals. As was observed earlier, our identities are bound up with these allegiances. One way that we register the requisite assurances is by expressing our negative attitudes toward those who do not share the group's perspective. We convey solidarity with our allies by punctuating our antagonism toward foes.

When we seek to uphold civil relations with our adversaries, we risk appearing inauthentic or disloyal to our allies. This can weaken our political alliances, thereby diminishing our political efficacy. What's more, given that our political allegiances are also central to our sense of individual identity, being regarded as disloyal by our allies often feels like self-betrayal. In letting them down, we fail ourselves.

These considerations show that the posture required by democratic citizenship is not only difficult to adopt; it is also morally strained. We are tasked with manifesting the attitudes and dispositions that express a due regard for our fellow citizens, even though this typically feels like a concession to injustice and a self-betrayal. Democratic citizenship imposes a *moral burden*.

Importantly, this burden is most imposing when the political stakes are high. When it comes to the political issues that we regard as most urgent, we place a correspondingly high value on achieving justice. This means that in such cases we assign a high moral importance to our political success. In a democracy, our political success is a matter of prevailing over our opponents. Under such circumstances, then, upholding the democratic ethos seems perverse. Engaging civilly with those on the other side *credits* them in some way. It therefore *empowers* them. In many other contexts, we would call this behavior *complicity*.

To repeat, active and engaged citizenship heightens this conflict. We are morally burdened by democratic citizenship *because* we take our responsibilities seriously. In striving to realize the democratic aspiration of a self-governing society of equals, we place ourselves in conditions that will prompt us to question whether we should sustain democracy. Indeed, we place ourselves in circumstances under which we are *right* to ask why we should sustain democracy. We bring the democrat's dilemma on ourselves.

## 4. Addressing the Citizen

That's the democrat's dilemma. It emerges from the perspective of the responsible citizen. Thus, the question of whether to sustain democracy arises in the course of the kind of political engagement that is required by democratic citizenship. More than this, it's often perfectly *valid* for a citizen to ask why she should sustain democracy. When the chips are down, it indeed might be best to treat politics as a cold civil war.

Although there are circumstances where citizens are permitted to withhold civility, it must also be the case that *not every* instance of high-stakes political conflict warrants the suspension of the democratic ethos. Otherwise, we would have no use for it. Hence there must be some cases where citizens are required to sustain democracy, despite the high stakes. Accordingly, even though I have presented the democrat's dilemma as a conflict that confronts engaged citizens, it also poses a problem for democratic theory. What reason can be offered in favor of upholding the democratic ethos? In the circumstances where citizens sensibly consider suspending democracy, what can be said in defense of sustaining it instead?

Though these are questions for democratic theory, they are not merely theoretical. It is important to formulate a response that *addresses* the citizen who is in the grip of the dilemma. The remainder of this book attempts this. In the coming chapters, I will argue that although the question of why we should sustain democracy is almost always worth asking, when we find ourselves in circumstances where we feel the pinch of the democrat's dilemma, we are also most likely to embrace distorted views of our opponents and their views. These distortions typically cast the opposition as more extreme, uncompromising, and disingenuous than they actually are. They lead us to assess our foes, inaccurately, as unreasonable. More importantly, though, I will argue that embracing distortions of our opponents encumbers our relationships with our allies. In other words, in succumbing to a distorted view of our political foes, we erode our capacity to collaborate effectively with our political friends. This, in turn, damages the prospects for achieving our political aims.

To start on this path, Chapter 3 examines the mechanisms through which earnest political engagement leads us to embrace exaggerated and inaccurate estimations of our political opponents and their views. The several mechanisms at work in this dynamic can be usefully captured with the single term "polarization." As this term is used in various ways by pundits and commentators, it will take some effort to make its meaning precise. With a clear view of polarization in place, the argument for sustaining democracy is relatively straightforward.

# 3

# The Polarization Dynamic

A few years ago, a student at my university invited me to participate in a campus debate organized by her sorority. Tennessee is a
capital punishment state, and the debate was to focus on whether
state executions should be televised. I was told that my opponent
would be a local attorney who opposes capital punishment and the
televising of executions. Prior to receiving the invitation, I hadn't
given much thought to the question of whether state-sanctioned
executions should be televised. However, I think that the state's
deployments of force generally ought to be publicly visible.
I explained to the student that although I also oppose capital punishment, I was prepared to argue in favor of televising executions.
I accepted the invitation.

The event was well attended and on the whole congenial. Yet
something was amiss from the very start. The attorney spoke first,
and his opening statement revealed that he was under the impression that because I would be defending the position that executions
should be televised, I must also support the death penalty. His case
against televised executions focused mainly on the injustice of capital punishment.

The arguments he offered against the death penalty were compelling, though conventional. However, the attorney's inference
from his opposition to capital punishment to his stance regarding
televised executions was surprisingly flimsy. His contention was
that support for the death penalty is always driven by cruelty, and
thus support for televising executions is a further manifestation
of that vice. His opening statement included the assertion that
my support for televising executions was evidence that I had been

"desensitized" to others' suffering. This alleged lack of sensitivity was projected as the explanation of how I could favor televising executions. Judging from the attorney's portrayal, only a moral monster could support the position I would be defending.

I hadn't realized that by participating in the debate I would be submitting to a stranger's pop psychological evaluation. In any case, the attorney offered no evidence in support of his claim about the psychological roots of what he took to be my view. I guess that those comments were intended as a strategic diversion, the kind of implicit personal insult that is permitted by the rules of formal debating and which can throw an opponent off his game. But who can say?

In any case, his opening comments had presumed that my support for televising executions was based in support for the death penalty. While he was completing his statement, I adjusted my opening remarks so that they called attention to his mistaken premise, emphasizing that my position was that executions should be televised *because* they are unjust. I then proceeded to sketch my case that a democratic citizenry that supports such a barbaric policy should not be able to shield itself from witnessing its enactment.

To my surprise, this argument stunned the attorney. He apparently had assumed that opposition to the death penalty *required* one also to oppose the televising of executions. All of his prepared remarks had been premised on the expectation that I would be defending capital punishment. He was driven to revise on the spot. Nonetheless, many of his contributions to the ensuing discussion retained the allegation that my view was at heart a manifestation of my cruelty. Even after he was compelled to acknowledge explicitly that we both object to capital punishment, the attorney proceeded to argue that my support of televised executions was nevertheless "indifferent" to the "barbarizing" of those who would tune in to watch them. He went so far as to suggest that this indifference was incompatible with full-throated opposition to capital punishment. The implicit suggestion was that my opposition to the death penalty was insincere or unprincipled. Anyway, my position didn't fit his script and the attorney consequently didn't have much to say in response to my arguments. As a result, the debate was a bit of a mismatch.

The attorney entered the debate with the attitude that there would be no room for good-faith disagreement between us. He accordingly sought to *diagnose* our difference rather than engage it. Of course, in attempting to diagnose our *disagreement* he only sought to diagnose his opposition. His preferred account cast opponents of his view, and thus me in particular, as psychologically derelict, or in the slightly more generous way he put it, "desensitized."[1] The exchange was consequently far less enlightening than it might have been. More importantly, however, he also seemed to have presumed that there could be no good-faith disagreement among allies, because true allies have nothing to disagree about. It was as if he believed that people must either agree on everything, or nothing at all.

Although this debate occurred a long time ago, I was reminded of it recently while catching up with a friend. In the course of chatting, she mentioned that she had just resigned from a small nonprofit organization she had helped to found that offers self-defense training to women. She told me that because demand for the training had grown significantly over the past year, the organization enlisted several new instructors. With the new instructors came a series of internal discussions about matters concerning gender identity, and a call for expanding the forms of training the organization offers. This was taken by my friend as a positive development, as she figured that the organization should seek to empower vulnerable people across the full spectrum of gender identification.

However, the expanded organization soon started fracturing. Some instructors began demanding that the group focus its training on economically disadvantaged districts of their city. Many instructors had been serving populations in affluent areas and were being pressured to discontinue those sessions. As many of the instructors lived in affluent areas and held full-time jobs outside of the organization, it was not feasible for them to establish a different clientele. They left the organization.

Other new instructors held the view that self-defense is only one dimension of a broader program of social empowerment. They pressed the organization to introduce training in resistance and de-arrest tactics designed for those engaged in political protest. As they saw it, the training should include the dissemination of information about local activist organizations. Still others saw the self-defense training as part of a more sweeping stance of nonviolence that includes opposition to the exploitation of animals and support for certain environmentalist ideals. They sought to introduce veganism and deep-ecology messaging into the workshops.

My friend said that the organization steadily devolved into an exhausting ideological struggle over the group's broader political aims and identity. This eventually drove its founding members to resign, not so much in opposition as in exasperation. In their absence, the group fragmented further. Internal tensions escalated among the different cliques, with each questioning the authenticity of the others' commitment to the organization's goals. The nonprofit is now defunct. The dynamic that led to its demise seems to have been roughly the same attitude as the one the attorney held: those who disagree about something don't truly agree about anything.

I won't draw any grand conclusions from these two vignettes. However, they bring into focus a few ways that sincere attempts to interact as democratic citizens can go badly. To put it very loosely, in order for political interactions to be fruitful, we need to understand one another, at least to a modest degree. Even when we seek to criticize or challenge others, the endeavor is futile unless we grasp their general stance. To that extent, we need to *cooperate* even with those whom we regard as our foes. We need to be able to accurately see where they're coming from. Similarly, if we are to work together with our allies, we need to have a rough sense of their perspectives regarding the aims and contours of the joint activity. Absent this rudimentary meeting of the minds, we find ourselves working at cross-purposes and our interactions fail.

In Chapter 2, I laid out how the democrat's dilemma emerges from within the perspective of the active democratic citizen. This chapter identifies the mechanisms that give rise to the dilemma. More specifically, I will show that the dynamics of political engagement can lead us to misconstrue one another in systematic ways, ways that cause us to embrace distorted views of others' ideas, concerns, and motives. When these misrepresentations are pronounced, we adopt demeaning attitudes toward our opponents. We come to see them as not only wrong about politics, but impaired as persons. We treat them as clinical subjects to be diagnosed rather than as our equals. This leads our opponents to adopt similarly negative assessments of us. In the end, our mutual misapprehension serves as a self-fulfilling prophecy. Each side comes to see the other as increasingly uncivil, and thus unwilling or unable to act as democratic citizens should. The challenge of sustaining democracy arises in a familiar way.

This chapter will also show that the same dynamics give rise to analogous dysfunctions in our political alliances. Partly because we are prone to regard our political commitments as aspects of our social identities, we tend to project onto our political allies an exaggerated degree of homogeneity. We expect them to be just like ourselves. This leads us to regard divergence from our expectations as a signal of their inauthenticity or disloyalty. The stance we take toward those whom we perceive to be counterfeit or lapsed allies tends to be more intensely negative than the one we adopt toward our outright foes.[2] We ask why we should uphold the democratic ethos with poseurs, merely *apparent* allies. The democrat's dilemma once again emerges. However, in this case, its source lies in the nature of political collaboration among like-minded allies. When we engage solely with our political friends, we can fall prey to dynamics that transform them into enemies.

There is a sense in which this is old news. In politics, opponents often miscomprehend one another, passing like ships in the night. It's also typical for allies to miss the forest for the trees. In the course of their collaborations, they lose sight of their larger purposes, allowing their alliance to splinter into tiny factions. These are among the ordinary pathologies of politics. What matters at present, though, is to see how these familiar pathologies can originate in political activities that are proper for democratic citizens.

The key to understanding these dynamics lies with the idea of *polarization*. This term may be familiar to you. A recent commentator claims that polarization is the "master story" of what's going wrong with democracy.[3] But if polarization is to be anything more than a *story* about democracy's troubles, we need to explain what it is. More specifically, we need to see how distinct phenomena, all of which are called polarization, impact our political thinking.

It is useful to begin by distinguishing two phenomena that are commonly run together: *political* polarization and *belief* polarization. The first is a measure of the degree to which different groups are opposed to one another. The second has to do with members of the same group. This distinction provides a more precise account of the threat that polarization poses to democracy. That account will help identify a prevalent mechanism that gives rise to the democrat's dilemma, which in turn will indicate why we should sustain democracy.

## 1. Political Polarization

The term "polarization" typically refers to the *ideological distance* between two or more political groups, whether they be parties, factions, constituencies, or some other unit.[4] When polarization in this sense is pronounced, the common ground between the opposing sides recedes, leaving no basis for cooperation, compromise, or even productive communication. When this occurs in decision-making contexts, the result is predictable: stalemate, deadlock, and animosity.

Call this *political* polarization. Political polarization is frustrating, as it's clear that democracy must get things done if it is to flourish. Political polarization can be dangerous, too. Inaction and inefficiency are often costly. Amid the partisan squabbling and gamesmanship, we still need a government that can *govern*. In a democracy, governing must involve cooperation and consultation across political divides. Political polarization thus seems to create conditions under which democracy cannot even commence, let alone thrive.

However, democracy sets the conditions for ongoing political disagreement. When such disputes occur within the bounds of what we earlier called good-faith political disagreements, they are a sign of democracy's health. The problem posed by political polarization cannot simply be the undeniably exasperating impasses and logjams—these are inevitable in a democracy. To grasp the difficulty that political polarization presents for democracy, we need to look beneath the surface of the phenomenon.

## 1.1. Three Sites of Political Polarization

I have said that political polarization is a matter of the ideological distance between two or more opposed political groups. Fair enough. But the idea of "ideological distance" is vague. I need to unpack this notion by distinguishing three different ways of construing it. These make for three different *sites* of political polarization.

One way of thinking about the ideological distance between opposed groups is to look at the differences among their official doctrines. In the case of political parties, this is relatively easy. We can look to their *platforms*. This allows us to say that two parties are politically polarized to the degree that their platforms are opposed or in some other sense incompatible. Let's refer to this species of political polarization as *platform* polarization.

Some degree of platform polarization is unavoidable in a democratic society. If there are multiple political parties, they must be distinguishable by their policy objectives. That political parties embrace opposing platforms might even be considered healthy. It shows that citizens have distinct political options, and thus that elections matter. Of course, platform polarization can become excessive, as when one party immovably wants the opposite of what the others want, or strictly *defines* itself as the opposition. In such circumstances, there is no basis for policy compromise or cooperation. Unbreakable deadlocks ensue. We can say, then, that platform polarization as such is not problematic, but it can become problematic when it escalates to a degree that makes government unworkable.

Consider a second way of construing ideological distance. Instead of examining official party documents, we could look at party leaders and official members. Here we can measure the ideological distance between opposed groups by looking at the degree of unanimity among the members of each. Opposed groups are highly polarized in this sense when their respective memberships include few moderates or bridge-builders. As it focuses on party leaders and official members, call this *partisan* polarization.

Partisan polarization is marked by the marginalization or even expulsion of group members who are willing to cooperate with the opposition. It typically is accompanied by the attitude that cooperation with the other side constitutes a kind of disloyalty. Accordingly, when partisan polarization is pronounced, political groups valorize uniformity and ideological purity. Often there develops a vernacular for calling out moderates, ridiculing them as inauthentic or disingenuous.[5] Under pronounced partisan polarization, moderates are either abandoned or sidelined, leaving only hard-liners to represent the group. The result is deadlock, but it is accompanied by cross-partisan hostility among leaders and official members.

Next consider a third way of understanding ideological distance. Rather than looking to party platforms and official members, we can examine the attitudes prevalent among ordinary citizens who identify with a political party.[6] *Popular* polarization is a condition where rank-and-file citizens embrace negative attitudes and dispositions toward those whom they perceive to be politically dissimilar from themselves, whether they be officials or fellow citizens. As it fixes on the attitudes citizens take with respect to their perceived political opponents, popular polarization need not track any actual policy divides.[7] Rather, citizens are polarized in this sense simply in virtue of their animosity toward those they regard as their political adversaries.

The data here are remarkable. In the United States, popular polarization has escalated markedly over the past four decades, despite the fact that divides over key policies have either remained stable or eased.[8] In other words, partisan citizens dislike those on the other side more intensely than ever, even though they are not significantly more divided over policies. Importantly, these citizens do not only report high levels of *dislike* for affiliates of the opposing party. They also incline to see them as untrustworthy, unpatriotic, corrupt, and dangerous. This leads them to regard their political rivals as threatening to democracy and thus divested from the democratic ethos. In addition, this animosity is directed at *fellow citizens*, not only the opposing side's candidates, officials, and spokespersons.[9]

This negative affect toward perceived political opponents is also *generalized*. We do not dislike those on the other side only for their politics—we also find their nonpolitical behavior disagreeable. The clothes they wear, the vehicles they drive, the food they eat, their preferred modes of entertainment, their pastimes, and more are all sites of cross-partisan contempt.[10] It may come as no surprise, then, that in the United States popular disapproval of interpartisan marriage is now more pronounced than disapproval of interfaith or interracial marriage.[11] Perhaps this is for good reason, too: co-partisanship is the most reliable predictor of long-term relationship success among those paired on online dating platforms.[12] In short, our partisan commitments have expanded into entire lifestyles, "mega-identities."[13]

Again, this escalation of popular polarization has occurred in the absence of correspondingly intensified divisions over policy.[14] To be sure, partisan citizens *believe* that their policy differences with the other side are extreme and expanding.[15] They attribute sharply opposing political ideas and values to those who affiliate with other parties. Yet these projections are generally inaccurate.[16] Relative to the prevailing levels of animosity, the actual divisions among rank-and-file citizens are slight. At the very least, they are no more severe than they were back when popular polarization was far less intense.

## 1.2. The Three Sites as Mutually Reinforcing

Heightened levels of popular polarization can explain the pervasiveness of partisan and platform polarization. When citizens intensely dislike those outside of their own political tribe, partisan polarization is incentivized among politicians and party leaders. Their job is mainly to win elections, and they do this by garnering support among their base.[17] To be more precise, in order to achieve electoral success, parties and officials must extract political behavior from their supporters; they must motivate citizens to donate, canvass, volunteer, and vote.

As it turns out, animosity, distrust, and other forms of negative affect aimed at the opposition are motivationally potent.[18] When citizens are deeply divided by negative affect for the other side, candidates and officeholders thus do well to amplify their unified animosity toward their opposition. This in turn rewards parties for adopting platforms that punctuate their differences from their opposition. In short, widespread popular polarization provides candidates and parties with a clear political strategy: demonize the opposition, valorize intransigence, feed partisan animosity. The three sites of political polarization thus reinforce one another.

Here's the upshot. Popular polarization is what renders partisan and platform polarization toxic. That is, in the absence of significant popular polarization, the other sites of political polarization can be kept within manageable limits. But when the citizenry is divided by intense negative affect, parties and officials need to escalate accordingly. In fact, we can see that intense popular polarization is *good* for political parties in that it provides them with straightforward electoral and campaigning strategies.

This is unsettling news for democracy. Not only does political polarization incentivize legislative deadlocks and political grandstanding, but it also promotes attitudes and dispositions that run contrary to the democratic ethos.[19] When popular polarization is prevalent, citizens come to regard their opponents as obstacles to be surmounted and threats to be neutralized rather than as partners in the shared enterprise of self-government among equals. In seeing the other side as divested from democracy, they divest, too.

Interestingly, citizens in the United States appear to realize the danger of political polarization. Across the partisan spectrum, citizens agree that democratic politics has become too noxious.[20] They say they want more cooperation and civility from politicians. However, they also tend to lay the blame for political antagonism squarely on their political opponents. They see the *other side* as overly disruptive, ruthless, and aggressive. Accordingly, they claim that the way to repair democratic politics is to insist upon greater *capitulation* from the other side. Note what's happening here: decrying political polarization is *itself* an expression of cross-partisan animosity, and condemnations of the polarized state of our politics are themselves affirmations of popular polarization.

These circumstances are bleak and, I suspect, all too familiar. So, the next question is why political polarization is so prominent. In particular, we must ask why popular polarization has come to be so widespread. To understand this, we need to examine the second kind of polarization: *belief* polarization.

## 2. Belief Polarization

Belief polarization affects the internal makeup of groups. It occurs *inside* them. Belief polarization is not a measure of the ideological distance between opposed groups, though, as we'll see, it plays a role in explaining how this distance can increase. It is rather a metric of what might be called an *ideological shift* that occurs over time within like-minded groups.[21]

Specifically, belief polarization is the phenomenon by which interactions among like-minded people tend to result in each person adopting more radical versions of their shared views. It is the force by which engagement with like-minded others transforms us into more extreme versions of ourselves. In this sense, belief polarization exhibits patterns more popularly known as the "yes-man" and "groupthink" phenomena: when we surround ourselves only with others who reinforce our ideas, we tend not only to become more confident in the correctness of those ideas, but also to adopt more radical or exaggerated formulations of them.

This shift brings a corresponding alteration in the ways we understand the basis for our beliefs. In the course of belief polarization, we come to overestimate the weight of the evidence that counts in favor of our views. We also become more dogmatic, that is, less responsive to counterevidence and criticism. We more readily dismiss and demean detractors, casting them as irrational and benighted. We become less likely even to listen to those who do not share our ideas, and more prone to interrupt them when they're speaking.[22]

Typically, the like-minded others who surround us are in the grip of similar forces. So we tend to fuel one another's escalation toward extremity. As we each adopt more extreme beliefs and attitudes, we also become more disposed to act together on their basis. As the shift initiated by belief polarization involves an escalation of *confidence* in our beliefs, we also grow more inclined to engage in risky behavior on behalf of our ideas. All the while, our views of those outside our group grow more intensely negative.

Belief polarization is surprisingly common.[23] It has been extensively studied for more than six decades and found to be operative within groups of all kinds, formal and informal. Importantly, belief polarization does not discriminate between different kinds of belief. Like-minded groups polarize regardless of whether they agree upon banal matters of fact, matters of personal taste, or deep questions about value. What's more, the phenomenon operates regardless of the explicit *point* of the group's interaction. Like-minded groups polarize when they are trying to decide on an action that the group will take, but they polarize also when there is no specific decision to be reached. Finally, the phenomenon is prevalent regardless of group members' nationality, race, gender, religion, economic status, and level of education.

In short, the phenomenon does not vary significantly with any of the expected demographic and sociological factors. As I said, it's a surprisingly robust tendency. It might be a good idea, then, to catalogue a few belief polarization experiments.[24]

## 2.1. Examples of Belief Polarization

One of the earliest experiments was conducted in France in the late 1960s. The subjects were asked to discuss both their (variously positive) views about French leader Charles de Gaulle and their (variously negative) views about American foreign policy. The individuals emerged with more thoroughly positive views of de Gaulle and more intensely negative views of American foreign policy than those they held prior to the conversation.[25] At the same time, the political attitudes of the group became more homogeneous.

In another early experiment, Michigan high school students were sorted according to their degree of racial prejudice. The like-minded groups then were tasked with discussing several issues concerning race in the United States, including the question of whether racism is the cause of the socioeconomic disadvantages faced by African Americans. Following the conversations with their respective groups of like-minded others, those who antecedently showed a high level of racial prejudice came to embrace more ardently the view that racism is *not* responsible for the disadvantages faced by African Americans, while those antecedently disposed toward low levels of racial prejudice grew more accepting of the view that racism is the cause of such disadvantages. Once again, discussion among like-minded people amplified pre-discussion tendencies. Accordingly, the ideological distance between the groups also expanded.[26]

A similar experiment involved adults who on the basis of an initial screening were classified into mixed-gender groups according to their views concerning the social roles of women. Once sorted into "feminist" and "chauvinist" groups, each discussed among themselves the merits of various statements about the role of women in society—statements like "A woman should be as free as a man to propose marriage" and "Women with children should not work outside the home if they don't have to financially." The result was that members of the feminist discussion group became more pro-feminist.[27]

In 2005, a sample of Coloradoans was sorted by an initial screening into "liberal" and "conservative" groups. Each group was then asked to discuss policies over which liberals and conservatives tend to divide clearly, including same-sex marriage and affirmative action. After the discussions, attitudes toward same-sex marriage and affirmative action underwent belief polarization: liberal support intensified, while opposition among conservatives grew more resolute. Importantly, the shift in group members' attitudes also resulted in a greater degree of internal homogeneity. That is, after discussion, not only did the members of each group tend to shift to a view more extreme than the one each person held prior to the discussion, but attitudes within the group also became more uniform. Each person shifted into a more extreme version of his or her prior self *and also* became more like the others in the group.[28]

Thus far, I have focused on the ways in which belief polarization initiates a shift in our beliefs and attitudes. However, as I mentioned earlier, belief polarization can also lead subjects to engage in more resolute and risky behavior on behalf of their commitments. Several experiments have shown this.[29]

In mock juries considering punitive damage awards, when jury members are initially agreed that the harm is severe and damages should be awarded, their deliberation produces a verdict of a significantly larger award than any individual juror's initial pre-deliberation assessment. The same goes for juries whose members are initially inclined to think that the harm in question is not particularly extreme and only a low degree of punishment is in order. After deliberation, the verdict is more lenient than individual jurors' initial inclination.[30]

Another study found that group discussion of an event that participants agree constitutes a serious violation of justice—sex discrimination committed by an elected official, for example—leads to a greater inclination among the discussants to engage in organized protest. What's more, among discussants who saw the violation as especially egregious, the enhanced readiness to protest was accompanied by a willingness that exceeds their pre-discussion inclination to protest in ways that are overtly militant and thus riskier.[31]

Add to these findings a few others that are more humdrum, but perhaps for that very reason all the more intriguing. A group of people who agree that a particular celebrity is attractive will report finding the celebrity significantly *more* attractive after they discuss the matter together.[32] Of course, the same holds for negative evaluations of faces: those who agree that a particular face is especially *unattractive* shift toward a more intensely negative assessment of the face after discussion. Another experiment showed that when people who agree that a particular dentist chair is especially comfortable get together to compare notes, they emerge with significantly higher estimations of its comfort.[33]

These examples might suggest that the phenomenon occurs only when matters of value or taste are under discussion. However, several experiments show that the phenomenon can be induced even with respect to strictly empirical or factual matters. Consider that subjects who agree that a particular city is notably high above sea level will adopt increasingly exaggerated assessments of its elevation in the course of discussion together.[34] To repeat, belief polarization operates regardless of the *kind* of belief that the group holds in common.

This is only a modest sampling of an extensive empirical literature documenting belief polarization. This catalogue should suffice, however, to demonstrate how common the phenomenon is. Drawing on these findings, researchers have appealed to belief polarization in explaining high-profile instances of group behavior gone wrong, including the Johnson administration's decision to escalate the Vietnam War, the risk-taking at NASA that arguably led to the *Challenger* explosion, and certain failing investment trends among otherwise highly successful financial groups.[35]

It would be easy to continue cataloguing experiments that document the belief polarization phenomenon. We need not pursue this further. My aim has been to identify the general dynamic that typically is set in motion when we collaborate with like-minded others. To summarize, such interactions tend to have the following effects:

- Individuals adopt more extreme beliefs and have greater confidence in them.

- Individuals become more like other members of the group in their beliefs and attitudes. Like-minded groups accordingly become more homogeneous.
- Individuals and groups grow more disposed to engage in risky behavior on behalf of their beliefs.

The phenomenon is striking. On occasions when I've discussed belief polarization with those not already familiar with it, some have reacted as if they found it to be some kind of magic spell. Yet belief polarization is less astounding than it might seem.

After all, we're familiar with other contexts in which group dynamics affect individual behavior. Peer pressure, rumor-mongering, guilt trips, fashion trends, "canceling," and viral internet memes are ordinary examples of ways in which we behave in coordination with specific others. We get a better sense of the belief polarization phenomenon by looking at the ways in which thinking is a kind of group behavior.

## 2.2. Thinking in Groups

It usually feels as if our thinking occurs somewhere inside our skulls. Nonetheless, we most commonly think in groups. Sometimes the group setting is overt. We talk things out, consult, share, brainstorm, and collaborate with others as a way of making up our own minds or coming to a firmer sense of our ideas. We turn to preselected others for confirmation and encouragement. And we occasionally seek out those who can be expected to criticize our ideas, using them as sounding boards so that we might devise better ways to articulate our ideas. Sometimes we even change our minds as a result.

There also are less explicit ways in which our thinking proceeds by way of others. For example, we often take the word of strangers whose judgment we trust. In some contexts, we look to those who have relevant experience that we lack, accepting their views as our own. We defer to experts; we consult data. And even when we seem to be thinking in seclusion, we commonly imagine how others might react to our ideas. We envision a devil's advocate, or we stage imaginary dialogues with friends and critics. As a result, when deciding where we stand on important questions, we typically think in a group, either explicitly or implicitly. In either case, our thinking largely depends on what others think.

This much is commonplace. Yet it is important to observe a different sense in which we think in groups. Thinking in groups also involves thinking *through* them, thinking *by means of* our social affiliations. As I noted in Chapter 2, we reflexively seek agreement with those whom we take to be our friends and allies, revising and adjusting our ideas so that they more closely fit with theirs. Although we usually do not instantly fall in line with the prevailing beliefs and attitudes, we try to avoid being too far out of step with those whom we regard as our peers. What we think is a reflection of what they think. In this sense, thinking is a group activity.

In thinking along with our peers, we also think *against* the identities of rivals. This is especially pronounced when we're thinking about evaluative matters, questions about how things ought to be. In such cases, we seek not only to come to the correct beliefs, but also to promote what we believe to be right. Accordingly, given our instinctual desire to stay in step with peers, there emerges within groups an intensified need for members to establish clear lines of distinction between themselves and members of opposing coalitions. We punctuate our distinctness from the out-group. And it is sometimes by means of this opposition that groups come to forge a more stable identity. We come to define ourselves largely in terms of what we oppose. What we are is what we're against.

In this way, deciding what to think is often a matter of figuring out who we are.[36] This in turn involves identifying with a peer group and, to some degree, internalizing their defining stance. However, where our group stands depends in part on the positioning of the groups it takes to be its rivals. Even before we make up our minds about an issue, we tend to have a sense of whom we agree with.

This is as it must be. Individual cognitive resources are limited, and the world is complex. We cannot help but rely on the minds of others, and thus we cannot help but think in, through, and against groups. Although it may *feel* as if thinking goes on somewhere in our own heads, in fact thinking about almost anything occurs within a complex web of social and cognitive interdependence with others. Formulating, maintaining, reporting, and revising beliefs and attitudes are to this extent group behaviors. Belief polarization is not magic at all. It rather is a predictable upshot of our inescapable cognitive interdependence.

## 2.3. How Belief Polarization Works

Aspects of belief polarization still seem mysterious. One might wonder why our cognitive interdependence drives us always to more *extreme* beliefs and attitudes. Why don't like-minded groups just as often shift toward more *moderate* commitments? Noting that belief polarization is both widespread and the product of our social and cognitive interdependence raises the question of how it works. What is the *mechanism* by which interactions with like-minded others transform us into more extreme versions of ourselves?

Two competing views immediately suggest themselves: the *informational* account and the *comparison* account. We'll look at each in turn. Then, finding each insufficient, I will develop a third option.

According to the informational account, discussion with like-minded others exposes us to a high concentration of affirming reasons and ideas and relatively few countervailing considerations. Consequently, group members absorb the new information, and revise their own view in light of it. People tend to exaggerate the weight and significance of new reasons that support the views they already hold, so as the new information confirms what they already think, they become more extreme advocates.[37]

Although the informational account surely captures part of what drives belief polarization, it cannot be the entire story. For one thing, belief polarization can occur in groups even when no new information is presented. In fact, it has been found to occur even in contexts where group interactions involve no exchange of information at all.[38] Although information exchange within like-minded groups might be a reliable way of initiating belief polarization, it is not necessary for it.

This suggests an alternative: the comparison view. This account holds that belief polarization results from in-group appraisals. Group members care about how they are perceived by the other members. In the course of discussion, they get a feel for the general tendencies within the group, and, wanting to appear to others neither as a halfhearted outlier nor as an over-the-top fanatic, they update their opinions so that their view lies notably above what they perceive to be the mean, but beneath what they regard as unacceptably hard-line.[39] Now, given that group members are engaging simultaneously in this kind of recalibration, the tendency to escalating extremity is to be expected.

Although it has clear advantages over the strictly informational view, the comparison account is still lacking. Just as belief polarization can occur in the absence of the exchange of information, it also can be induced in the absence of in-group comparisons. That is, group members can shift even in the absence of any kind of interaction with other members that would allow them to compare and calibrate their beliefs.[40] Again, although comparison within a like-minded group might be a reliable channel through which belief polarization initiates, it is not necessary. A third account is needed.

Thus, the *corroboration* view. It says that belief polarization is driven by our internal estimations of the dominant tendencies within our identity groups. More specifically, the relevant shifts occur simply in light of group-affiliated *corroboration* of one's views. We shift into more extreme versions of ourselves as a result of feeling that a group with which we identify widely shares a view that we espouse. We need not hear any reasons in favor of the view, nor need we be in the presence of other members of the group with whom can compare ourselves. Instead, the realization that one's view is *popular* among one's identity group is enough to initiate belief polarization.

The thought behind the corroboration view is that belief polarization is driven more by group affinity and thus *affect* than by information or evidence. However, as it recognizes that exchanging information and performing in-group comparisons are often ways of situating oneself within a group of like-minded others, the corroboration view need not deny that the other accounts capture particular ways in which belief polarization occurs. In other words, the corroborationist claim is not that information exchange and in-group comparisons are irrelevant, but only that the deeper mechanism driving the phenomenon has more to do with the positive affect that results from the affirmation of one's identity group. Accordingly, this view draws on the idea that corroboration from our peers makes us *feel good* about our shared beliefs, and this makes us feel *affirmed* in our group membership, our social identity. When we feel elevated in this way, we shift toward extremity.

This leads us to an additional thought. Much of the experimental literature on belief polarization naturally involves face-to-face discussion among like-minded people. This has encouraged the idea that the phenomenon occurs centrally by way of discussion. The corroboration view helps us to see that although discussion within like-minded groups is a reliable context for studying belief polarization, the paradigmatic site for the phenomenon lies elsewhere—namely, the stadium.

## 2.4.  Belief Polarization and the Stadium

If you're a sports fan, recall the last time you were in an arena packed with fellow fans as your team was winning an important game. You probably arrived for the game in attire that signaled your allegiance to the team; you thus dressed in a way that makes you look more like the other fans of the team. As the team played, you cheered and rooted along with the others—standing, sitting, applauding, singing, and so on in unison with them. There might have been an official team mascot on the field who occasionally cued group behavior.

As the team scored, your enthusiasm intensified. You came to see new merits in the team's players; your estimation of the team elevated. Moreover, you came to more fully *identify* with them; you began to feel more strongly that their victory was also your victory. You became more of a fan. And there's a good chance you left the stadium having purchased additional merchandise that expresses your allegiance to the team.

That's not all. In the course of the intensification of your enthusiasm for the team, you probably also came to adopt an elevated sense of the importance of their winning. It started to feel as if their loss would be some kind of wrong or calamity. This corresponded with a deepening sense of alienation from the opposing team and its fans. The other team came to look more unskilled, and their fans began to seem pathetic and misguided, perhaps even detestable. This is partly why, when our team's winning, we regard it as the result of their superior skill, but when they're losing, we look to factors like cheating, deficient refereeing, and plain old bad luck instead of the merits of the opposition. In any case, in the course of an important game, our negative feelings toward the opposing team and its affiliates are intensified. You probably know someone who can't stand the *thought* of wearing a rival team's jersey. This person probably also regards the fans of a rival team as personally disagreeable. Now you know why.

If sporting events aren't your thing, a similar account can be given with respect to just about any other context where people with allied loyalties assemble to express them together. Rock concerts, comedy shows, religious revivals, and, of course, political rallies all are ready examples. Note also that these gatherings share a similar structure. These days, political rallies and religious revivals are designed to *feel like* rock concerts and pro football games.

Full exploration of these similarities would carry us too far afield. The point is that although the extremity shifts that characterize belief polarization can be induced in various ways, they are the result of the elevation of affect that comes from the corroboration of our allies. To repeat, we shift toward extremity because positive affirmation from those we see as relevantly similar to ourselves makes us feel good about who we are and what we believe.[41] This elevated self-assessment leads to greater confidence, which in turn encourages the expression of more extreme commitments and a greater willingness to act.

Recall that corroboration need not involve the introduction of any new *evidence* in favor of one's view. It's simply a matter of being affirmed by others with whom one identifies. As this suggests, corroboration can come by way of highly indirect channels. One need not be *in the presence* of others to feel affirmed in the relevant way. For example, presenting a subject who identifies as liberal with a chart showing that liberals widely oppose genetically modified food can prompt belief polarization. Similarly, exposure to a poll showing that conservatives overwhelmingly favor a particular military action can produce an extremity shift in the belief content of a conservative already favorably disposed to that action.[42]

It is important to note that the operation of belief polarization is often unnoticed. We rarely *recognize* the intensification as it is taking place; in some contexts, we tend to *deny* that any shift has occurred.[43] As we shift toward extremity, it feels as if we're simply expressing the attitudes we have held all along. When we are in the grip of belief polarization, our more extreme selves strike us as our true or genuine selves. The expression of intensified affect thus feels like authentic self-expression. Consequently, although we readily recognize it in others, and especially those whom we see as rivals, our own vulnerability to belief polarization typically escapes our notice. For that reason, we also tend to overlook it in our allies.

An intriguing implication follows. The social environment can trigger belief polarization. These environmental prompts need not be verbal, overt, or literal; they can be merely implicit signals to group members that some belief is prevalent among them. Accordingly, hats, pins, campaign signs, logos, gestures, songs, and roughly any environmental feature that makes salient a social identity and the attitudes that are common to it are all potential initiators of belief polarization for those who share that identity.[44]

Chants, catchphrases, slogans, emblems, and the like are important markers of political identity. They are also reliable signals to like-minded others of the extent to which the group's ideas and sentiments are widespread. Think of this next time you see that your neighbors have placed dozens of identical campaign signs on their front lawn, or when a candidate publicly insists that a rally was more widely attended than has been reported. The aim of these measures is to give the *impression* that the candidate is popular. And, largely because of how belief polarization works, convincing people that something is popular is a reliable way of making it popular. In this respect, large-scale politics is no different from marketing.

## 2.5. Polarization as a Dynamic

We have been examining belief polarization because we seek to understand a puzzling feature of contemporary democratic politics in the United States: partisan animosity among citizens has intensified significantly in recent decades despite there being no proportional increase in political divisions over concrete policies. We dislike the other side more intensely, and we are more thoroughly convinced that our differences are irreconcilable, while in fact we are far less divided than we suppose. In other words, what we earlier called popular polarization is rampant, despite the fact that political divides among rank-and-file citizens are no more severe than they were forty years ago. The severity of our political divides is partly a *projection*. The question is why.

The corroboration view of belief polarization provides an explanation. Recall the observation from Chapter 2 that we *identify* with our politics. We see our political views as more than beliefs that we hold; they are more like commitments that make us who we are. Taken collectively, our opinions function like a political *stance*, what we earlier called our *conception of justice*. This is part of the reason we often talk about politics in ways suggesting that we *are* our views. We identify *as* our partisan allegiance and hence situate ourselves socially by means of our politics. In this sense at least, politics is thoroughly *personal*.

Additionally, more and more of what we do these days is regarded as expressive of our political allegiances. Especially in the United States, partisan identities have become "mega-identities," amplified into lifestyle differences.[45] Politics has *saturated* the whole of social life. Accordingly, everyday behaviors increasingly have a political valence, which invites interactions with certain people while deterring others. This has resulted in a broad partisan sorting of social spaces. Again, liberal and conservative citizens systematically live in different neighborhoods and homes, shop at different stores, do different kinds of work, worship in different congregations, vacation in different locations, express different aesthetic sensibilities, and so on.

As the country as a whole has grown more diverse, the local spaces that citizens inhabit have become more politically homogeneous.[46] Our daily routines, then, tend to place us in social interaction only with those who share our social identity and thus our politics. Even when these interactions are casual and not explicitly about politics, our partisan identities are so central to our overall sense of ourselves that our political commitments are nonetheless corroborated. This exposes us to belief polarization.

Belief polarization affects our attitudes and dispositions toward others. As we transform into more extreme versions of ourselves, we also come to adopt increasingly negative stances toward those we perceive to be different. As we shift toward a more extreme position, opposing views begin to look all the more disfigured, unfounded, and irrational. Those who hold such views start to look to us as ignorant, naive, and malign. Moreover, as we shift toward extremity, we come to regard our opponents as uncompromising extremists. As we grow more distant from them, we see *them* as shifting beyond the pale. We accordingly lose the ability to recognize nuance in their perspective: we ascribe to them only the most exaggerated formulations of their views, and we come to see them as a fanatical monolith. We hence grow distrustful of them, increasingly inclined to fault them with being lazy, unpatriotic, unintelligent, immoral, and treacherous.[47]

In the end, once belief polarization has set in, even relatively amicable interactions with our political opponents tend to further our extremity. Calls to "reach across the aisle" backfire.[48] Ironically, as we come to regard our opponents in these ways, we come to more fully fit the description that we ascribe to them. Often, they're subject to the same forces. A tragically self-fulfilling projection results: each side becomes their opposition's most unflattering caricature.

This shows how belief polarization and political polarization work together in a degenerative spiral that can be called the *polarization dynamic*. As we shift into more extreme versions of ourselves, we also adopt increasingly negative attitudes and dispositions toward our political opponents, eventually seeing them as incompetent, depraved, and untrustworthy. They begin to appear to us more as obstacles to be overcome than as our political equals. Accordingly, attempts at civility and cooperation begin to look Pollyannaish, if not positively complicit. The basis for regarding those with whom we disagree as nonetheless our fellow citizens, each entitled to an equal say, recedes. We hive together in like-minded enclaves, plotting ways to prevail over our enemies. This initiates further belief polarization, which in turn produces more popular polarization. The other side behaves in much the same way. And, as we observed earlier, when popular polarization is widespread, parties, candidates, and officials are incentivized to punctuate their differences, demonize their opponents, escalate hostilities, and initiate standoffs.[49] And on it goes.

Once again, it should be emphasized that these attitudes and tendencies are more pronounced in citizens who are politically active. Democratic citizenship hence faces a kind of self-defeat. Our earnest attempts to fulfill the responsibilities of citizenship expose us to forces that instigate belief polarization, which in turn fuels the polarization dynamic. As a result of our political engagements, political differences with our opponents more frequently occasion the democrat's dilemma. Our conception of the spectrum of reasonable views shrinks. So, too, does our sense of when good-faith disagreement is possible. Even though citizens are actively engaged in the project of self-government in ways that are commendable, democracy nonetheless can devolve into a cold civil war.

## 3.  Polarization Among Allies

The aim of our inquiry is to develop a compelling reply to citizens who are confronting the democrat's dilemma. In the course of their political activities, they come to suspect that their opponents are insufficiently invested in the democratic ethos. When the political stakes are high, citizens who regard their opposition in this way are warranted in asking themselves why they should uphold civil relations with them. Why not instead simply work to overcome the other side? Why should they sustain democracy?

I have identified a prevalent mechanism by which even sincere and well-motivated political engagement can distort our impression of our political opponents. In leading us to more extreme attitudes and commitments, belief polarization draws us to misconstrue opposing ideas and the people who espouse them. We come to see opposing views as uniformly extreme and implausible, while also over-ascribing negative traits and motivations to our foes. Eventually, political opposition as such looks unreasonable. This initiates the polarization dynamic, which reinforces a range of democratic dysfunctions. Democracy seems fated to unravel.

Perhaps we ought to embrace the conclusion that democracy really is civil war by other means, hopefully less bloody ones. One might say that we needn't sustain democracy, because the aspiration for a society of self-governing equals is fundamentally incoherent: in the course of democratic participation, citizens will inevitably come to regard those with whom they disagree as less than their political equals. Is that where the argument leads?

I don't think we should draw this conclusion. At least not yet. Seeing why will take a little more work. The discussion thus far has emphasized the ways that belief polarization affects our own beliefs and attitudes, and thus our conceptions of our opponents. What we have yet to explore is the way that belief polarization can distort our relations with our *allies*.

## 3.1. Love Your Political Enemies?

To start, consider a common reaction to the trouble posed by the polarization dynamic. Some democratic theorists claim that the lesson of the polarization dynamic is that we must learn to love our political enemies, that we must work to appreciate that they're not as terrible as we think. This thought is often accompanied by the claim that democracy depends upon a broad consensus of value and overall community among citizens. Those who endorse this view then say that the polarization dynamic only goes to show how fragile democracy is when it is not rooted in a common way of life.

The solution, then, is to dismantle the polarization dynamic by cultivating community.

In one sense, this is a reassuring response. The polarization dynamic indeed leads us to overstate our differences and adopt exaggerated views of our opponents' defects and flaws. It's true, after all, that our political foes typically are not as bad as they seem. Surely democracy could use a little more concord and goodwill, too. So why get all worked up about politics? Just relax! The solution to the problem of sustaining democracy thus seems clear. We simply must eliminate partisan animosity. Love your political enemies, and eventually you'll see that they're not enemies after all.

Whatever the merits may be of loving your political enemies, this is not the resolution I propose. It's important to explain why. That the polarization dynamic leads us to exaggerate our divides does not entail that our actual political differences are trivial. Similarly, that we are no more divided today over policy than we were forty years ago does not mean that we are not significantly divided.

More generally, my view is that our political differences are real, and they matter. Part of what it means for them to matter is that they provoke partisan conflicts and hostilities. These differences typically are focused on crucially important values, such as justice, liberty, autonomy, and dignity. These values matter, and we should consequently expect disagreements about them sometimes to grow heated, tense, and adversarial. However, when such disputes are well managed, they nevertheless serve as affirmations of one another's political equality. Democracy is the proposition that a relatively just and decent social order is possible *despite* ongoing and often antagonistic disagreements about these important things.

The "love your political enemies" solution is really a dodge. It poses no response to the democrat's dilemma at all. If we are going to supply citizens with sufficient reasons to sustain democracy with their opponents, we must begin from the premise that partisan hostility and conflict are inextricable from the democratic endeavor.

Some of your fellow citizens are, indeed, not your political friends. They're your political enemies. That's democracy.

## 3.2.  Fractured Allegiances

Return to the basic phenomenon of belief polarization. As groups undergo belief polarization, their members shift into more extreme positions. But remember that groups also become more homogeneous. That is, as groups undergo belief polarization, members become both more extreme *and* more alike. Crucially, the resulting homogeneity is not limited to their shared commitments. With belief polarization, group members become more alike across an expanding range of attitudinal and behavioral dimensions.[50] They become more like one another almost across the board.

Here's why. As was noted previously, our partisan political allegiances have inflated into entire lifestyles. They have saturated our social lives, extending deeply into aspects of social life that are arguably not matters of partisan politics. Accordingly, almost anything we do these days is understood to be a way of enacting our political identity. We *express* to others our partisan allegiances by driving a particular kind of vehicle, carrying a reusable water bottle, wearing a red baseball cap, eating a particular kind of fast food, buying organic vegetables, and even pronouncing certain words with an unfamiliar accent.[51] Our political identities are central to our overall self-understanding, so these behaviors are instances of self-expression. They are public affirmations of who we are, signals to others of where we stand.

As a result, our political allies come to *expect* these behaviors from us. And as out-group hostility escalates, deviation from our own group's expectations can signal disloyalty or inauthenticity, leading to marginalization or expulsion. In short, as groups experience belief polarization, they not only become more homogeneous; they also become more *conformist*. In order to maintain good standing with one's allies, it is typically not enough to affirm the prevalent beliefs and attitudes. One must also affirm one's authenticity as a group member. This means that one must express attitudes and commitments that satisfy the expectations of one's allies across an expanding range of behaviors.

Think again of sports fans. Even when not in the stadium, they tend to dress in the apparel of their team. They commonly display emblems and other symbols of their allegiance to the team on their cars and personal effects, as well as in their homes and workspaces. Moreover, they share common attitudes and dispositions with fellow fans, including negative assessments of rival teams and their fans. When fans gather together on game day, these tendencies are of course amplified. As a result, group cohesion becomes all the more important. To deviate from the other fans' expectations is hence seen as a defect; to show an insufficient degree of enthusiasm is to fail the team and thus to be subject to reproach by other fans. No one wants to be labeled a poseur by one's allies.

The important thing to emphasize is that none of this behavior *feels* like conformity. Fans have internalized the group identity. So, fitting in with other fans of the team feels like self-affirmation. Wearing the same colors, displaying the same symbols, expressing similar attitudes, acting in concert, and other modes of satisfying group expectations are forms of authentic self-expression, not compliance. In behaving like the other fans, each fan enacts their true self.

Things are not that much different when it comes to our political allegiances. In fact, many of the more troubling aspects of fandom are amplified in the political context. Our partisan identities have grown progressively more encompassing—we regard more and more of what we do as expressive of our political allegiances. Accordingly, the range of behaviors that call for compliance with group expectations expands. Because we tend to see the stakes as far higher in politics, we also place greater import on group cohesion and, thus, poseur detection. And when it comes to politics, we are prone to adopt more intensely negative attitudes toward those whom we see as insincere or lapsed members of our group than toward those whom we see as our opposition. From the perspective of our partisan identities, inauthenticity is more contemptible than outright error, and treason is a more serious offense than outright heterodoxy.[52]

When poseur detection becomes paramount in the life of a group, the coalition must devise clear standards of authenticity. The members must be able to gauge one another's investment in the group's identity. This means that the group must rely on consolidated and strong leadership to provide the necessary signaling regarding group expectations. Consequently, as groups undergo belief polarization, they not only become more homogeneous and conformist. They also become more internally hierarchical and thus less egalitarian.

Note the implication. Belief polarization renders our political coalitions more insistent on across-the-board alignment with the group's expectations concerning an expanding spectrum of behaviors. This means that they also become less accepting of differences among group members, even regarding behaviors that arguably are not relevant to the political objectives of the group. Because these expectations are set by group leaders, we can say that when belief polarization occurs in groups, they become internally less democratic. But that's not all. As the pressures of authentic allyship escalate, belief-polarized groups manifest a local form of partisan polarization as well; they marginalize noncompliant members, and gradually expel them. Consequently, coalitions shrink, leaving a membership composed solely of uniform hard-liners.

In short, belief polarization fractures our alliances, shrinks our coalitions, promotes hierarchy within our collaborations, and transforms political allies into foes. This is bad news for the democratic ethos. But it's also bad news for our political commitments, our aims for justice. After all, if we are to prevail politically in a democracy, we need to build and maintain coalitions. This means that we must maintain our capacity to collaborate with those who share our objectives. So, we have to preserve the ability to work on shared goals despite looming sites of deep disagreement. As it intensifies our sense of the importance of widespread in-group cohesion, belief polarization counteracts these competencies, thereby undercutting our efforts on behalf of our political commitments.

Recall the self-defense organization that was discussed at the start of this chapter. The instructors were allied with respect to the objective of providing self-defense training to women. Yet they also embraced incompatible conceptions of the broader nature of their shared endeavor. These differences eclipsed the common ground among them, leading to infighting over their differences. But the members didn't see themselves as imposing supplementary demands on one another; instead, each regarded their larger vision of the group's work as capturing the true essence of its mission. Each saw any member who resisted their conception of that mission as a fake, a counterfeit member of the group, someone deserving expulsion. In the midst of all the conflict, the founders of the organization all stepped aside, leaving only hard-liners, who ultimately proved unable to keep the organization afloat.

This is admittedly an exaggerated case. However, my guess is that certain features of the self-defense group's demise will be familiar to anyone who has helped to build a political coalition. When organizing for collective action, it is crucial that members' investment in the endeavor remain high. The group must remain focused and motivated. In political contexts, this often means that group members fix on the flaws of the opposition, reminding themselves of what's at stake should the other side prevail. Again, negative affect toward the other side is a reliable motivator of political behavior.[53]

Although negative feelings aimed at the opposition are potent, they invite danger. When we regard our opponents as depraved extremists who are undeserving of engagement and thus must simply be overcome, we disengage from them. This leads the forces of belief polarization to turn inward, driving our coalition to splinter into distinct hierarchical factions, each developing its own conception of the larger identity of the coalition, each therefore doubtful of the others' authenticity and commitment.

As a result, a small-scale polarization dynamic is initiated. The internal factions adopt hard-line stances and intensify internal pressures to conform. Cooperation with those outside the faction is demonized as complicity or disloyalty. Moderates and bridge-builders are expelled. In-group hostilities escalate, and power struggles emerge. The larger coalition unravels, and, amid all of the internal struggles, the group's initial objectives go unmet. It's as if we need to maintain civil, albeit adversarial, relations with our political enemies in order to pursue justice.

## 4. The Dilemma Resolved: Why Sustain Democracy

Isn't it ironic? The democrat's dilemma arises in cases where it seems to us that treating our opponents as our equals impedes justice. Yet this very stance winds up undermining our political objectives. To recall how this works, let's rehearse a familiar line of reasoning: We see the opposition as advocating policies that are out of step with what justice demands, and this leads us to conclude that sustaining democratic relations with them only gives them an undeserved political advantage. It then strikes us that by suspending democracy with them, we improve the chances of achieving justice. Hence, our zeal for justice occasions the democrat's dilemma. It supplies a compelling rationale for the claim that we should indeed suspend democratic relations with our opponents.

But this reasoning is flawed. The very same zeal for justice that motivates us to suspend democracy with our foes also heightens our exposure to belief polarization, which leads us to overstate our opponents' vices and to inflate our reasons for regarding them as divested from democracy. Moreover, we have seen that once we have disengaged from our opposition, belief polarization works to dismantle our capacity to recognize good-faith disagreement among our *allies*. Our political coalitions thus devolve, which also damages the prospects for achieving justice as we see it.

That's the irony. Our sincere dedication to justice can backfire. Insofar as it occasions the democrat's dilemma, it heightens our exposure to belief polarization. This in turn encourages attitudes and dispositions that ultimately render us less efficacious political actors. Further, belief polarization erodes our democratic capacities. As it progresses, we become less capable of regarding those with whom we disagree as our equals. It additionally causes us to overinflate the significance of disagreements among our allies. When belief polarization is pronounced, we are left unable to cooperate on civil terms with anyone who isn't just like us. Our political endeavors thus lose their democratic cast; in seeking to *prevail* over our opponents, we attempt to *impose* what we regard as justice on our fellow citizens. Accordingly, a deeper irony looms: our zeal for justice can transform us into exactly what our worst enemies say we are.

A response to the democrat's dilemma now emerges. Thus far, I have been looking at the dilemma as if it were strictly focused on our political opponents. We ask why we should treat them as our equals, given that justice is at stake. This way of construing the problem is understandable, as the dilemma is indeed occasioned by our interactions with political foes. However, this chapter has shown that the case for sustaining democracy lies elsewhere.

Sustaining democracy is not really about our adversaries after all. Not centrally, at least. It's about our friends, our allies, and the political aspirations that we share with them. In a nutshell: We need to sustain democracy with our enemies if we are to sustain democracy with our friends. We need to uphold democratic relations with our reasonable opponents if we are to maintain the capacity to treat our allies as our equal partners in the pursuit of justice.

Here's a more detailed formulation. Sustaining democracy with our foes is necessary in order to manage belief polarization. Managing belief polarization is necessary if we are to preserve our political alliances and keep them internally democratic and efficacious. But the forces of belief polarization are not sensitive to who our friends and foes are. In the absence of engagement with political opponents, belief polarization turns inward. It shifts toward our coalitions, sowing divisions within them that easily escalate into fractures. Again, when our alliances devolve in this way, not only do we become less effective politically, but our own democratic capacities devolve as well. We begin to see all opposition as unreasonable, all opponents as uncivil, and every disagreement as in bad faith. We lose the ability to regard anyone who isn't just like us as our political equal. We become uncivil. We come to fit our opposition's distortions of us. When we opt to suspend democracy, we jeopardize our own democratic capacities.

Hence there is a grain of truth in the simple response to the democrat's dilemma that was dismissed early in Chapter 2. Treating our political opponents as our equals is, indeed, a matter of justice. Justice demands that we sustain democracy. But the reason for this is not as straightforward as the simple response supposes. When we withhold civility from our opposition, we impair our ability to pursue justice with our allies. Although this consideration may appear to invoke a merely instrumental reason for sustaining democracy, the argument is also moral. It is a *moral* requirement to try to maintain conditions under which justice could be achieved. Consequently, since justice is what matters, we have a reason to sustain democracy with our adversaries.

Of course, this is not to say that all of our political opponents are at heart decent democratic citizens who are *deserving* of civility. That belief polarization leads us to exaggerate our rivals' vices does not entail that they are always virtuous. Consequently, the argument does not deny that sometimes our opposition is, just as we suspect, malicious, corrupt, and disingenuously committed to democracy. Indeed, we often have good reason to think that some particular rival contingent is merely playing at democracy, seeking to encourage us to adopt democratic norms only so that they can subvert them and thereby gain political advantage. Under such conditions, we must find a way to sustain democracy without adopting a Pollyannaish view of the other side. Thus, the next question: how can we do this?

# 4

# How Can We Sustain Democracy?

In the months leading up to the 2016 presidential election in the United States, I conducted an informal experiment about political opinions. You probably recall that the electoral contest between Hillary Clinton and Donald Trump was especially acrimonious and unrelenting. Gaffes and purported scandals dominated the headlines. Each candidate routinely declared the other to be fundamentally unfit for the office of president. Early in his campaign, Trump adopted the additional posture that Clinton was a criminal whom he would "lock up" if he was elected. He went so far as to threaten Clinton with jail on national television during one of their debates. By anyone's standard, it was an especially ugly chapter in US politics.

I reside in a region of the country notorious for the unassuming sociability of its people. Perhaps for this reason casual chat about the latest political news was at that time inescapable. A trip to the grocery store or gas station could easily turn into a political summit among strangers. These conversations would typically begin with an implicit reference to the latest gaffe or misstep—"Can you believe what Hillary did?" or "Did you hear Trump last night?"—and then progress into a discussion of the relative merits of the candidates, the latest polling, and the state of democracy. These conversations often focused on the demeanor and character of the candidates. They commonly would develop into expressions of indignation and outrage. Many people expressed political exhaustion and a corresponding wish for the election to be over. Only very rarely were the candidates' official platforms and policy commitments mentioned. And when these were mentioned, they rarely went beyond the candidates' slogans.

Maybe because I was raised in a region of the country that is not known for friendliness among strangers, I instinctively sought to curtail such interactions. At first, I adopted the strategy of politely nodding affirmatively to whatever was said until my interlocutor took the hint that I wasn't interested in a discussion of politics. But with the release of the *Access Hollywood* tape where Donald Trump bragged about committing sexual assault and Hillary Clinton's slightly earlier "basket of deplorables" remark, I found that my nodding was almost always taken as *encouragement*, a solicitation for my interlocutor to go on. As the nodding was also often taken as an expression of *like-mindedness*, I sometimes would be subjected to statements of escalating antagonism toward whomever the speaker took to be their political opposition. It was uncomfortable.

I resolved to take a different tack. Whenever someone would strike up a conversation by saying something like "Did you hear that Trump tape?" or "Did you hear what Hillary called Republicans?" I decided to respond by saying "Yes, but I haven't decided yet what to think about it." I had figured that this response would signal a general lack of interest in carrying the discussion further, thereby saving me from the need to politely nod in response to whatever was coming.

Alas, it was a mistake to think that this new response would have that effect. In fact, it was *naive*. My reply almost invariably prompted further discussion. It was most frequently taken as a request for more information, and thus as an invitation for the interlocutor to continue. *You're not sure what to think? Bless your heart. Let me help you!*

The follow-up discussions were revealing. In nearly every instance in which I confessed to not knowing what to think about the latest campaign news, my interlocutor assumed that I wasn't fully informed about what had happened. My claim that I wasn't sure what to make of, say, Hillary Clinton's "basket of deplorables" remark was taken as a confession that I either *did not know* what she said or *hadn't fully grasped* its significance. After I said "I'm not sure what to think about that," typically I would be briefed on the incident in question. As one might expect, although my interlocutor would present the report as a simple retelling of the facts, it would almost always conclude with a *judgment* with which I was expected instantly to agree, such as "She's a horrible person."

I would normally respond to the summary verdict with a statement like "Well, maybe—but I'm still thinking about it." This reply was often taken as a social cue that I did not want to pursue the discussion. In many instances, the topic was dropped and the interaction ended. Sometimes the discussion would conclude with an expression of mildly apologetic bewilderment at my response— "Okay, I was just letting you know"—but, by and large, the exchanges closed amicably.

Yet there were also cases where things ended on a less pleasant note. My "I'm still thinking" response to the recapped campaign news was at times taken as a *rejection* of the interlocutor's description, an expression of doubt about whether the episode had been accurately conveyed. Thus I often heard a reply like "No—that's *literally* what she said." In many of these instances, my uncommitting response was frequently understood to be an affront, as if I had implicitly expressed an opposing verdict. So, to stay with the example of Hillary Clinton's statement about "deplorables," my response was sometimes met with an escalating comment designed to antagonize. In one memorable exchange, a person told me, "Well, she's an elitist, and I see that you probably are, too." In a similar encounter, I was told that indecision about Hillary's comment was equivalent to condoning what she had said. Another time, an interlocutor expressed relief that Clinton had "finally called the Republicans what they are." I hesitatingly responded that, as I understood it, her comment was not directed at Republicans as such but only at certain Trump supporters. To this my interlocutor said, "But these people *really are* deplorable; if you won't acknowledge that, I'm wasting my time talking to you." Southern kindliness goes only so far.

A different occasion punctuated an additional dimension of many of these episodes. A cabdriver brought up the *Access Hollywood* tape. When I said I hadn't decided what to make of it, she said, "Well, all it shows is that Donald Trump has a potty mouth . . . of course, the media's making a big deal out of it. But it's nothing." She then went on to explain that there was a recording of Trump using "bad words." But she hadn't mentioned what Trump had said. As I was stuck in the cab and couldn't break off the conversation easily, I responded that to my knowledge, what people were objecting to was not Trump's choice of words, but rather the fact that, by speaking as he did, he demeaned women, humiliated a particular woman as she was doing her job, and bragged about committing sexual assault. The driver replied, "We'll have to agree to disagree there."

The driver understood my account of what people in fact found objectionable about Trump's statements to be an affirmation of their assessment of the incident. As far as she was concerned, in *reporting* that some claimed that the tape revealed something more troubling than Trump's "potty mouth," I had taken the side of Trump's opponents. My attempt to clarify that I had simply reported what some found objectionable about the tape was met with no response: the driver had stopped talking to me. The conversation had ended once I gave voice to an account of the facts that ran contrary to the one that she favored. This was probably for the best.

This was an experiment only in an extended sense of the term; these anecdotes do not support any far-reaching conclusions. But they bring the next step of the argument into focus. Having seen in Chapter 3 *why we should* sustain democracy, we now need to discern *how we can* sustain democracy. To be clear, in asking *how we can* sustain democracy, I am not raising the question of whether one can *muster the will* or *bring oneself* to do it. That's a question of motivation. The question I'm addressing is *practical*. I want to identify *what we need to do* if we are to sustain democracy. What steps can we take?

One might think that sustaining democracy is a straightforward endeavor. Chapter 3 drew the conclusion that it is largely a matter of managing belief polarization. So, one might reason that because belief polarization arises out of strained relations among political opponents, managing it is centrally a matter of repairing or reconstructing those relations. This is admittedly an intuitive idea. Additionally, easing cross-partisan tensions is a worthy enterprise. But I will argue here that this way of understanding the task ultimately sets us on the wrong path. The key to managing belief polarization lies elsewhere.

To be more specific, I will argue that managing belief polarization is a matter of reorienting our relation to our own political commitments, of seeing them—and thus ourselves and our allies—in a different light. In this way, sustaining democracy does not aim strictly at fixing our political divisions or bridging partisan divides. It's not *directly* focused on those things, at any rate. Rather, sustaining democracy poses a fundamentally *internal* challenge. It is a challenge that lies within us and among our coalitions.

I admit that these claims are vague. It is the job of this chapter to clarify what they mean. But before launching into the thick of things, it will be helpful to linger a bit longer on the political interactions described earlier. They reveal important features of political identity that must be accommodated in our account of how we can sustain democracy.

## 1. The Depth of Political Identity

My informal experiment suggests a few reassuring upshots. Across the board, these are cases of individuals acting as citizens and aspiring to take citizenship seriously. They regarded the election as *public business*, something to be discussed openly, even with strangers in informal settings. The assumption driving the encounters is that individual political judgments matter and thus are appropriate topics of casual public discussion among citizens. Moreover, the people I spoke with took themselves to be politically informed. They were eager to share political news and exchange ideas, at least up to a point. Accordingly, my claim not to have decided what to think about the episode in question was never taken as an expression of my lack of interest in politics. My indecision was seen as something to be remedied, rather than simply passed over. For the most part, my interactions were courteous, even when they were slightly awkward. They never turned aggressive or overly nasty, even in the cases where my interlocutor took me to be a political foe. So far, so good.

Yet these interactions also demonstrate that not all is sweetness and light. Daniel Patrick Moynihan is credited with the observation that although we are all entitled to our own opinion, none of us is entitled to our own facts. In these exchanges, my interlocutors understand the facts as *necessitating* an opinion, an instantaneous judgment about the broader significance of the facts. Accordingly, my claim to not know what to think about the latest campaign episode was nearly invariably taken as an implicit admission that I hadn't really understood what had happened. In almost every case, my interlocutor proceeded as if I only needed to be told the story in order to decide what to think. The assumption seems to have been that simply being presented with the facts would be enough to elicit a determinate judgment.

This is why in several instances, the person I was talking with found my irresolution confounding. Those who did not know my political leanings took my indecisiveness as placing me on the side of their opposition; from their perspective, then, my indecisiveness was disingenuous. Those who assumed that I was a political ally saw my withholding of judgment as unintelligible. For them, it was as if we were at a sporting event together, and when our team scored a goal, I claimed to need a moment to decide whether to cheer.

In both kinds of case, the assumption was that one shouldn't need time to digest the facts, because facts speak for themselves. More than this, my interlocutors seemed to hold that facts always speak decisively in favor of some particular partisan conclusion. In the tenser interactions, my interlocutor appeared to hold that *understanding* the political episode in question meant simply agreeing on the spot with their specific judgment about it. Even though I had explicitly claimed that I *was still* thinking, my withholding approval of their assessment of the facts was taken to entail that I had rejected the facts themselves. They seemed to have reasoned that, by resisting their judgments, I demonstrated my obtuseness and perversity, my refusal to accept plain facts. As one interlocutor put it, it's a waste of time to talk politics with someone who won't acknowledge facts.

In short, the idea that politics calls for reflection and judgment had been abandoned. From the perspective suggested by my partners in these interactions, politics really is a matter of aligning one's political instincts with the goals and interests of the party with which one affiliates. On such a view, political thinking requires little more than standing prepared to reflexively evaluate political matters in ways favorable to one's partisan allegiances. Thus, the ground for disagreement within one's coalition recedes, as does the possibility of agreement with those who embrace a different political identity. There can be no critics among allies, and no accord with foes.

The troubling implication should be evident. It was argued in Chapter 2 that good-faith political disagreement is both the by-product and the nurturant of democracy. Yet when political facts are understood to be inevitably packaged in partisanship, the possibility of such disagreement is jeopardized. After all, if political disagreements are to be in good faith, they must proceed against the backdrop of some shared basic conception of *what is at issue* in the dispute. When the facts themselves are taken to be incipient articulations of our favored partisan conclusions, this common ground dissolves. When this happens, there can be no good-faith political disagreement. We simply talk past one another in ways that reinforce our mutual animosity. All that's left of political discourse is the clash of partisan appeals, a battle conducted not with arguments, but with opposing catchphrases, mottos, innuendos, and smears. When it is reduced to this, politics inevitably becomes a matter of partisans preaching to their respective choirs about the depravity of those outside the congregation. Along the way, the very idea that politics presents us with something to *think about* is jettisoned, replaced with slogans that overtly cast reflection as necessarily being political obstruction or even a kind of injustice: "Silence is violence"; "There is no middle ground"; "Neutrality is complicity"; "Either you're with us or you're against us."

Under these conditions, civility in our sense—the disposition to formulate one's political views in ways that account for the concerns and objections of one's opponents—is hardly possible. Instead, misunderstanding, distrust, animosity, and resentment are encouraged, and these in turn provide additional fuel for the polarization dynamic. Note once again that the entire cycle is driven largely by earnest and sincere democratic engagement. The problem, in other words, is *internal* to democracy.

## 1.1. Some Experimental Findings

Thus far, I've been extrapolating on a few anecdotes. However, it turns out that these casual observations comport with experimental findings. As was noted earlier, citizens in the United States largely agree that politics has grown too hostile and adversarial. Across the spectrum of partisanship, they indicate that they would like to see greater cooperativeness and cooperation among politicians and parties. Yet citizens also tend to lay the blame for current levels of political intransigence and animosity squarely with their political opposition.[1] That is, citizens tend to see their opponents as the sole cause of the dysfunctions.

That's not all. Our perceptions and evaluations of others' behavior are colored by our partisan identities.[2] Recall that when we experience belief polarization, we come to ascribe political significance to an increasing range of behaviors. This of course applies to perceived allies and foes alike: as we shift into our more extremely partisan selves, behaviors ranging from driving a particular kind of vehicle (hybrid or pickup?) to wearing a particular kind of apparel (camo or yoga?) or consuming a specific brand of coffee (Starbucks or Dunkin'?) come to be seen as partisan indicators, ways of identifying others as political allies and foes. These behaviors then become ways in which we publicly *express* our political loyalties.[3] We wear the camo shirt or drive the hybrid car as a way of *signaling* our political allegiances to others. In short, across an expanding range of action, we see in one another's behavior the avowal of partisan identity. Along these lines, one experiment finds that we tend to be forgiving, or even condoning, when our allies engage in political behavior we generally disapprove of—such as stealing the opposition's campaign signs off the lawns of their supporters—even though we remain strongly condemning of our rivals when they act in kind.[4] Among our allies, the act expresses a message we endorse. When performed by our rivals, it signals a commitment we oppose.

This is part of a broader tendency to assign intentions, motives, and dispositions to others based on what we perceive to be their partisan identity.[5] Note, too, that the attribution of positive traits to co-partisans and negative traits to perceived opponents extends across the board. We regard co-partisans as *more reliable* sources of information about nonpolitical matters with respect to which they have no special expertise than political opponents who are also experts in those areas. For example, one study finds that we assign higher reliability to co-partisan testimony about how to fix a car than to the testimony of political opponents, even when the opponent is an accomplished auto mechanic and the co-partisan has no expertise with automobiles whatsoever.[6]

We also are unlikely to allow those we perceive to be political opponents to *correct* us, even when it's clear we've made an error that they're well placed to detect and remedy. In fact, when a perceived political opponent corrects us, we incline to double down on our initial error.[7] Along similar lines, exposure to even moderate expressions of opposing political opinions tends to further entrench polarized attitudes toward opponents.[8]

## 1.2. Political Identity as a Way of Seeing the World

These observations and experimental results suggest a striking conclusion about just how deep political identity runs in our sense of ourselves. Recall that our political opinions express an overall, though often only implicit and somewhat ad hoc, conception of justice. Although our conceptions of justice are often far less systematic than we suppose, we nonetheless identify with them. We *see ourselves* in our ideas about how the political world should be. Politics is in this sense always personal.

Yet this is not to say that politics is always *individual*. We identify ourselves by way of our social affiliations and loyalties. We find ourselves by locating those with whom we belong. These days, our political ideas are most commonly organized around the platforms and values of large-scale national political parties. We therefore have come to identify increasingly with our partisan allegiances; we see ourselves as our party affiliation. Politics is personal, but it is nonetheless also communal.

Meanwhile, our partisan affiliations have extended their reach beyond politics, saturating every aspect of social life.[9] Liberal and conservative citizens in the United States today occupy different, and quite separate, social and physical environments. They live different sorts of lives. In short, as partisan affiliation has moved to the center of how we understand ourselves, it has also become more than a strictly *political* identity.[10] Our partisan identity places us within a political social sect, with its own social and physical spaces that curate our everyday experience. This suggests an even deeper layer of political identity: in addition to being personal and communal, politics also is *tribal*.

Political identity runs so deep that it functions as a *way of seeing the world*.[11] As our political identities are entrenched tribal lifestyles, they in part establish and depend upon tribal rivalries. Regarding our political opposition as an alien and enemy tribe is a way of affirming our authentic membership in our own. Our views about our rivals hence come largely from our allies. And this means that our conceptions of our rivals tend to be exaggerations and distortions. We come to regard any common ground with them as illusory and suspect. Eventually, the only people whom we can interact with productively are those who see things as we do.

Hence, my cabdriver was wary of conceding that critics of Trump were objecting to something other than the vulgarity of his words. She implicitly understood that to see the issue as involving anything other than his choice of words would welcome an untoward conclusion, so she resisted the attempt to describe the event in a way that might lend itself to that result. She and I parted ways on the *description* of what the outcry was fundamentally about. In a way, she was justified in breaking off the conversation where she did.

Similarly, the Hillary Clinton supporter took my unwillingness to endorse her "deplorables" remark as evidence that I was possibly one of the deplorables, and in any case not worth talking to. From his perspective, Clinton had at last articulated the deep truth about Republicans, and anyone who needed to step back and evaluate what she had said was merely preparing to backpedal. That Clinton's statement was referencing a particular element within Trump's base rather than all Republicans was a minor detail, worthy of examination only if one was aiming to side with the deplorables. Again, our dispute turned on a difference in understanding *what had been said* rather than the significance of what had been said.

Consider next the campaign sign stealers. One could say that our condemnation of the behavior when conducted by our opposition but not by our allies reveals an all too common variety of political hypocrisy.[12] But our account of partisan identity suggests that's too facile an explanation. Given our tendency to ascribe positive or negative traits and motives to others based on their perceived partisan identity, the case is better understood as indicating a difference in our perception about the act that was committed. To explain, when our allies steal the campaign signs of an opponent, we see them as serving justice. The act itself, then, is seen as but a minor infraction that is offset by the broader objective of securing a just result. However, when opponents steal the campaign signs of our allies, we regard them as serving injustice. In that case, the infraction of stealing another's property is compounded by the additional injustice of abetting a flawed political objective.

One might go so far as to say that in these cases, partisans *don't see the same event.*[13] They do not perceive that their allies are engaged in the *same behavior* as their opposition. When perpetrated by an ally, sign stealing is an act of mischief that furthers justice and is thus forgivable. But when an opponent steals a campaign sign, she is impeding justice and in addition defecting from democratic norms; she is thus guilty of a serious offense and deserving of condemnation. From the perspective of the partisan, the differential judgments do not reveal hypocrisy at all. The acts in question are of different moral kinds, and thus warrant different evaluations.

Imagine a confrontation between opposed partisans about an instance of campaign sign stealing. One sees the episode as an act in pursuit of justice that involved an excusable bit of mischief. The other sees the act as suppressing justice and violating democratic norms. Recall that they each *see* things in their respective ways. In this sense, their dispute emerges at the level of the *description* of the event in question.

How will they regard each other? Each sees the other's description of the event as a *distortion* of the facts, an instance of *spin*. Accordingly, for either to accept the other's description of the event would be to *contravene* their own evaluation of it. Unless they're able to place some distance between their partisan identities and the episode in question, they're bound to a kind of mutual incomprehension that escalates cross-partisan animosity. Each will see the other's depiction of the event as a con. Each will eventually come to regard the other as incompetent, untrustworthy, irrational, untethered to reality. More importantly, they will also see each other as uncivil and uninterested in having a proper discussion. This of course *confirms* their antecedent negative attitudes toward the other. The polarization dynamic is thereby accelerated.

George Orwell wrote that "to see what is in front of one's nose needs a constant struggle."[14] He was lamenting the ways in which powerful interests manipulate political information and thus constrain our political thinking. However, that the struggle to see clearly in politics is also due to forces within ourselves. Our partisan identities can drive our perceptions of political affairs, coloring our conception of basic facts as well as our attitudes and judgments. The task of managing belief polarization is more complicated than it might seem.

Specifically, we can't break the polarization dynamic simply by approaching our fellow citizens in a spirit of democratic open-mindedness, though doing so may of course be admirable. Consider a different way forward. One might argue that we should *expect* belief polarization to thrive in the social and political environment it has created. Perhaps the proper conclusion to draw is that democracy can be rehabilitated only with expert assistance.

## 2. The Facilitated Democracy Approach

Motivated by the dysfunctions I have been documenting in this book, some contemporary democratic theorists have developed a range of experimental programs for democratic revitalization that involve what can be called *facilitated democracy*. These proposals aim to repair political relations by encouraging citizens to participate in specially designed forums where, with the assistance of professional facilitators, they come together to gain information, share perspectives, exchange reasons, listen to arguments, and contribute to rendering a collective judgment, all under conditions designed to elicit democratic norms of respect, inclusion, fairness, and reciprocity.

Several models of facilitated democracy have been proposed. Some, variously known as deliberative polls, citizen juries, minipublics, and citizen assemblies, are highly institutional and designed for large-scale application. Others are more informal, seeking to revive community by way of relatively local civility and conflict resolution practices.[15] The differences between these need not concern us here. The important thing is what these programs have in common—namely, the idea that citizens can cultivate the virtues of democratic citizenship, and thus overcome democratic dysfunctions, by participating in processes designed to elicit their best civic selves amid political difference.

A great deal of encouraging research has emerged concerning facilitated democracy.[16] Some data suggest that participation in facilitated democracy events promotes mutual understanding among opposed partisans, increases individuals' understanding of political issues, and strengthens the inclination to vote.[17] Some find that collective decisions emerging from these events tend to be more rational and better informed.[18] Other research suggests that those who engage in these processes find the enterprise valuable, as participants tend to volunteer to take part in other events of this kind.[19]

This is all to the good. However, the data are not univocally positive.[20] Some researchers have found that engagement in facilitated political deliberation events has a *negative* impact on political participation. More specifically, some data suggest that participation in facilitated democracy *discourages* subsequent political participation.[21] Another study finds that a facilitated event *exacerbated* belief polarization among participants.[22] And some research finds that interactions under facilitated democracy conditions reinforce the antecedent negative stereotypes partisans had of their opposition.[23]

I do not need to weigh in on the conflicts among these findings. My point rather is that mixed data are to be expected. It is likely the case that those who enter into facilitated democracy events with positive expectations tend to find the exercise positive and indeed benefit from it, while those who bring different attitudes to the enterprise likely do not.[24] And my suspicion is that the difference between the two broad classes of participant has to do with the degree to which they have already gone through belief polarization.

This is where the limitations of the facilitated democracy approach come into view. It may be true that bringing citizens together to deliberate under the conditions modeled in facilitated democracy is a reliable way to *prevent* or *arrest* belief polarization. However, recall that the task is to *ease* and, to the degree it's possible, *reverse* it. Data suggesting that facilitated democracy events do not produce further polarization do not show that they *reduce* antecedent levels of polarization. To be sure, arresting belief polarization is part of managing it. But it's not clear that facilitated democracy has much to contribute to the broader aim of undoing the belief polarization that already exists among citizens.[25]

Consider a related concern. Grant that in facilitated democracy experiments, polarization does not intensify, mutual understanding increases, and participants become more favorably disposed to participate in politics. It remains unclear whether these improvements persist beyond the experimental setting. One must ask: what happens to participants' attitudes and dispositions when they are removed from the specially curated forum of facilitated democracy and placed back in the wilds of highly polarized democratic politics, where differences are not moderated by an expert facilitator?

Even if it is assumed that the benefits of facilitated democracy indeed *are* durable beyond the experimental context, this concern persists. This is because facilitated democracy participants will nevertheless confront a political scene in which most of their fellow citizens have *not* participated in facilitated democracy. Their political interactions therefore will be strained in the usual ways. Their efforts to uphold the norms of proper democratic interaction will not be reciprocated, and many of their political opponents will regard such efforts as underhanded and otherwise suspect. The democrat's dilemma thus eventually reemerges, along with the challenge of sustaining democracy.

Whatever its other merits might be, the facilitated democracy approach is not sufficient for managing belief polarization. It is important to note that its limitations are largely due to its underestimation of the depth of political identity. To see this, note that facilitated democracy treats belief polarization as primarily a matter of *information*. The assumption is that partisan hostility and other dysfunctions have to do largely with the fact that citizens bring different information and different levels of informedness to their interactions. When citizens begin from significantly different understandings of the relevant facts, their attempts to discuss their differences lead only to frustration, which escalates into incivility and distrust. Facilitated democracy interventions aim to repair this, first by breaking citizens' informational bubbles and supplying citizens with a shared understanding of the facts relevant to their differences, and then by encouraging orderly and reasonable discussion. As one theorist and advocate of facilitated democracy puts it, the point of the exercise is to provide a picture of democracy "when the people are thinking."[26]

Political identity runs far deeper than this. Moreover, belief polarization is driven by political identity. Belief polarization isn't driven strictly by *informational* factors, and partisan animosity isn't solely the result of hostile or frustrating interactions with political opponents. Rather, belief polarization is instigated by corroborations of partisan identity and fed by affirmation from perceived allies. The broader social environment is saturated with corroborating signals, so it is naive to think that exposure to diversified information in an experimental setting will ease belief polarization in the real world.

Again, our political commitments locate us within various alliances and partisan formations. These coalitions partly depend upon signals of allegiance among allies, which commonly take the form of expression of cross-partisan animosity. We exhibit the partisan attitudes we do in part because they are necessary in order to maintain our alliances. We assure our co-partisans that we are authentic and thus dependable allies by signaling to them our negative appraisals of the opposition. None of this can be eliminated from democracy—these phenomena are part of the profile of democratic citizenship.

The task of managing belief polarization thus is not simply a matter of staging more orderly and judicious interactions among political opponents. In fact, some research suggests that depolarization may have more to do with exposing partisans to the opposition's *reasons* in the absence of any actual interpersonal interactions.[27] To be clear, this does not amount to a *rejection* of the facilitated democracy approach. Rather, it shows that, at least in its current manifestations, facilitated democracy is *not sufficient* as a strategy for managing belief polarization. We have seen that its limitations are due to the relatively shallow conception of political identity that lies behind the interventions it proposes.

## 3. How to Sustain Democracy

We must look elsewhere for an account of how we can sustain democracy. But where? We appear to be in a bind. The fact that partisanship is so deeply entrenched in our self-understandings might threaten the very project of sustaining democracy. If everything we do is an expression of our partisan selves, any political intervention aimed at managing belief polarization is likely simply to exacerbate the trouble. It seems that the democratic ethos inevitably devolves, that democratic citizenship is indeed self-defeating. Perhaps the democratic aspiration is a delusion, and democracy can never be anything other than a cold civil war.

This is a dispiriting conclusion. Does the argument we have been developing lead to it? I don't *think* so. That is, I think it is *possible* for democracy to avert this grim fate. Still, showing that we have not painted ourselves into this particular corner will take some work. More specifically, it will take some imagination— conjecture that's rooted in existing empirical findings, but as yet still speculative.

Begin by noting a more general limitation of facilitated democracy. In treating political identity as shallow, the facilitated democracy approach focuses nearly exclusively on the *relations* between citizens. It locates the *site* of democratic dysfunction within the *interactions* among persons, particularly those who are politically opposed. Facilitated democracy aims to repair those interactions in line with properly democratic norms.

Rehabilitating citizens' relations with one another is the objective of sustaining democracy, too. Yet some goals can be achieved only *indirectly*—by attending to something else. At any rate, the depth of political identity points to a different site for the required intervention. As is typical in cases of impaired interpersonal relations, the rehabilitation of our associations as citizens requires that we work on ourselves. In order to manage belief polarization, we need to reorient our relationship with our political commitments. This means that the challenge of sustaining democracy lies within us. To make sense of this statement, let's start by saying what this thesis is *not*.

## 3.1.  What Sustaining Democracy Does
## Not Require

Let us return to fundamentals. Democracy is an antagonistic enterprise among political equals who disagree about justice and hold conflicting views about the general shape the political order should take. In some cases, these disagreements can be addressed with a principled compromise. But in other instances, any resolution of the impasse will strike at least one of the parties as a capitulation, a surrender, a rotten concession to injustice. Yet democracy involves the requirement that, even in these latter cases, citizens must regard their reasonable adversaries as political equals. Moreover, they must see their government as required to enact reasonable outcomes of proper democratic decision-making processes, even when they regard those outcomes as unjust. Unless the injustice is egregious to an extent that would warrant civil disobedience and other such measures, when confronting results of this kind, citizens must pursue democratic channels of effecting political change, from ordinary campaigning, canvassing, and social criticism to lawful forms of demonstration, protest, and dissent. In such cases, the cure for democracy's ills is more democracy.

This means that sustaining democracy *cannot* require citizens to step away fully from politics or stifle their political convictions. To recall language from Chapter 2, democracy is an aspirational ideal whose pursuit depends upon an engaged and contesting citizenry. Consequently, the project of sustaining democracy cannot be that of befriending one's political enemies or adopting the attitude that politics is too small to get agitated about. Nor can it involve the idea that democratic citizens must adopt a quasi-skeptical "who knows?" stance according to which their political opponents might in the end be correct. No, democracy needs citizens who hold *real* convictions and are ready to engage politically on their behalf.[28] Animated and adversarial, but nonetheless in good faith, political disagreement among citizens who have staunch convictions is part of the package of democracy. Any response to the challenge of sustaining democracy that calls on citizens to set aside their rivalry is a dodge.

For similar reasons, sustaining democracy is not the project of developing within oneself the disposition to uphold civil relations *despite* the opposition's overt rejection of democracy's ethos. Democracy depends upon *good-faith* political disagreement among citizens. Accordingly, to proceed civilly with those who will not reciprocate is ordinarily to surrender the democratic enterprise. Although there may be special cases where adhering to democratic norms in dealing with those who are at best nominally invested in democracy is advisable, this cannot be a requirement of the democratic ethos. In short, democracy cannot demand that we make ourselves easy targets for the strategic machinations of nondemocratic agents. Under ordinary conditions, then, unilateral adherence to the democratic ethos is not a way to sustain democracy.

In order to sustain democracy, we need to manage belief polarization within ourselves. Various disengagement and divestment strategies help to diminish the degree of conviction or fervor with which we hold our political beliefs. For that reason, they might be methods for managing belief polarization as such. But they nonetheless are not ways of sustaining democracy. They *cannot* be. Sustaining democracy is a matter of sustaining *democracy*, not something else. Even though the activities of democratic citizenship expose us to forces that can erode our capacities to fulfill our civic role, we remain democratic citizens, and thus must take responsibility for our politics. Consequently, in claiming that the project of sustaining democracy is *internal*, I am not preparing to recommend that we soften our political convictions and scale back our advocacy. The task of managing belief polarization calls for a different kind of reorientation.

## 3.2. Sustaining Democracy Within

*response*

I can now state things directly. If we are to manage belief polarization in ourselves, the first thing we must do is recognize the vulnerability of our political commitments to *reasonable criticism*. Remember the discussion in Chapter 2: *reasonable* criticism draws from concepts and values that are compatible with the fundamental ideals of a democratic society. Accordingly, reasonable criticism is not necessarily *decisive* or *formidable* criticism. It rather is criticism that cannot be simply dismissed as beyond the pale.[29]

We acknowledge that our political views are susceptible to reasonable criticism, at least *in principle*, insofar as we accept that they could be improved upon, clarified, and sharpened. In recognizing that our political ideas could be more precisely formulated or more clearly articulated, we acknowledge that, as they stand, our political ideas could be reasonably criticized. And we in fact tend to accept that our political views are improvable in these ways. We typically do not take ourselves to be infallible or to have reached our final political conclusions. Rather, we take ourselves to still have things to *learn* about politics, and we take *overconfidence* to be a political vice. We realize that we can gain a firmer *command* of our ideas, discover new ways to see how they fit with our other commitments, and discern stronger reasons for our general perspective. And even when we consider views that we regard as settled, we recognize the possibility of finding for them a more refined presentation, a more compelling rationale, or at least a better sense of how they can be misunderstood.

In this sense, we regard our political views as works in progress. This is not because we see ourselves as undecided or wavering; it is because we recognize better and worse ways of framing the ideas we hold. When we improve our ideas by sharpening the way we articulate them or fortifying the reasons we offer in their support, we do not thereby *change our mind* so much as gain a *firmer grasp* on our commitments. Criticism is the mechanism by which our ideas can be improved.

However, in order to *recognize* the vulnerability of our political views to reasonable critique in a way that can manage belief polarization, we need to do more than affirm the *in-principle* possibility of their improvement. We need also to affirm it *in practice*. We need to establish reminders to ourselves that our political commitments, no matter what their other merits may be, are not *beyond* such criticism. The way to do this is to seek out such reasonable criticisms and grapple with them. This will lead us to grow accustomed to recasting, refining, reformulating, and, if necessary, revising our political ideas. As a result, we can come to appreciate the varied merits of different ways of formulating the views we accept. We thereby develop a sense of the range of reasonable variation in ways of formulating and understanding our position. In other words, we will come to recognize that not everyone who resists our particular expression of our political views is for that reason a political *opponent*. We hence come to realize that there can be critics among our allies. In turn, we learn that there is a range of doctrinal variation among those who share our political identity.

Now expand the focus. When our allies also adopt processes of exposing their ideas to reasonable criticism, our alliances grow more accepting of doctrinal variation within the group. Members come to see other members as potential critics, but nonetheless devoted to *improving* the coalition's stance. We hence come to be more accepting of good-faith disagreements among our political partners. Our sense of the demands of authentic membership in the coalition loosen, becoming less exacting and less monolithic. We become able to disagree with our allies without calling their authenticity into question. This recognition of reasonable dissensus among allies can prevent the in-group dynamics of belief polarization that normally lead to fracture.

The proposal, then, is that we can manage belief polarization and thereby sustain democracy in ourselves and our alliances by taking steps to keep ourselves mindful of the fact that our political commitments are not beyond reasonable criticism. We can achieve this by actually subjecting our political ideas to reasonable criticism. A reliable way to do this is to engage with our political opponents, to actually go to the source and find out why they reject our views. This may sound simple, perhaps simplistic. Yet there are subtleties in the proposal that must be underscored. It will again be helpful to attend to what the proposal is *not* claiming.

First, note that the prescription is not that we all must strive to develop optimal formulations of our political opinions. I am not recommending that we seek out reasonable criticism because doing so enables us to better root out error and grasp the truth. One might strive for the truth, of course, but the proposal isn't focused on the *value* or *merit* of our political ideas at all. Rather, the claim is that if we hope to manage belief polarization, we must recognize *in practice* that our views are subject to reasonable criticism. We do that by actually exposing them to criticism of that kind.

More importantly, though, it should be emphasized that in recognizing that our political commitments can be reasonably criticized, we do *not* thereby adopt the attitude that our commitments might be incorrect. This is because views that are true can nonetheless be reasonably criticized. Recall that reasonable criticism needn't be especially *formidable* or *compelling*. What's more, even misplaced and failed objections can be instructive—again, they can show us the ways in which our views can be misunderstood or misconstrued. The attitude that our political ideas can be reasonably criticized thus is consistent with the assessment that they are correct.

For similar reasons, the proposal does not require us to admit that our opponents' views might be right or that the truth lies somewhere in between our position and theirs. The acknowledgment that our political views are subject to reasonable criticism does not prescribe a quasi-skeptical "I could be wrong" or a relativist "Let's see both sides" or "They might have a point" posture. Indeed, recognizing the possibility of reasonable criticism is compatible with unwavering and deep conviction. It concedes nothing to opposing views. The recognition of the possibility of reasonable criticism still permits one to maintain that the opposition's political ideas are demonstrably false and thus fit for wholesale rejection.

Accordingly, the proposal does not call for a retreat from adversarial political engagement, either. It does not recommend that we befriend opponents or socialize with those on the other side. It is, moreover, consistent with building tight-knit political coalitions for the purposes of initiating political change. Again, seeing our political commitments as subject to improvement by means of reasonable criticism does not preclude us from assessing our opponents' political objectives as incompatible with justice or otherwise morally flawed. And that our opponents hold political views that are misguided and even wrong does not render them incapable of raising important objections to our views.

That last point calls for elaboration. My proposal for sustaining democracy does *not* call for us to attend to the opposition's positive case for their views. The idea is *not* for citizens to expose themselves to the arguments in favor of the political views they reject. Nor is the prescription that we must always listen to the other side or endeavor to assume a neutral posture from which to evenhandedly weigh all perspectives on the issues we care about. Whatever their general merits might be, these measures can escalate belief polarization under existing political conditions.

We sustain democracy by occasionally stepping away from this kind of pro-and-con examination of the issues over which we are divided. The recommendation is for citizens to focus on *reasonable criticisms* of *their own* views, the reasons opponents find them less than compelling. The exercise is thus directed not toward hashing out which side is correct, but rather at getting a better sense of what one's opposition finds unconvincing, unclear, or insufficient about one's own view. In stepping away from the question "Who has the right view?" and toward the question "Why don't they agree with us?" the exercise aims at *improving* one's own political views, not weighing them against opposing positions with the aim of determining whose view is best. Remember, the claim is that managing belief polarization requires that we take steps to remain mindful of the fact that our political views are improvable in light of reasonable criticism.

Of course, none of this presupposes that our reasonable opponents have good reasons for rejecting our views. It is consistent with the idea that our political opposition is *misinformed* about our views or *misunderstands* them. Nor does the proposal claim that it's our duty to correct our opponents' misconceptions of our position. Although under certain circumstances it is a good idea to attempt to do so, it does not impose on us the chore of improving our opposition's understanding. Relatedly, the prescription is *not* to expose ourselves to opponents who would be abusive or threatening; nor does it require us to acquaint ourselves with criticisms that are, indeed, beyond the pale. The objective is to discern ways in which our views can be *reasonably* criticized so that we can grow more accepting of doctrinal variation among our allies.

The general spirit of the proposal for sustaining democracy within is captured somewhat in John Stuart Mill's claim that "he who knows only his own side of the case knows little of that."[30] Mill embraced the more sweeping idea that citizens need to confront one another in the kind of pro-and-con argumentation that the present proposal advises against. Nonetheless, Mill suggests an informal test that we might apply to ourselves when assessing how well we are doing at managing our belief polarization. We can ask ourselves questions like: What's the best reasonable criticism of our position? What does our best-informed and sharpest reasonable critic say is the most damaging weakness in our view? How is our position most commonly misheard by reasonable opponents? If we find that we are unable to answer these questions, or unable to formulate answers that identify *reasonable* criticisms, we should conclude that we are failing to manage belief polarization.

### 3.3. The Importance of Political Distance

So, the first step is to establish habits and practices that keep us mindful of the fact that our political ideas can be reasonably criticized. This gives rise to a second step that we must take.

My proposal for sustaining democracy relies upon a distinction between our opposition's *criticisms* of our views and their positive *reasons for their own* views. To be clear, the difference between these two kinds of consideration is not always easy to track. This is largely because the flaws in an opponent's view are among the reasons that count in favor of one's own. Yet *reasons for* and *reasons against* are distinct, at least insofar as the perceived defects in a given opponent's view do not by themselves determine which among its possible alternatives one should adopt.[31]

Although the distinction is often difficult to draw, we must keep it in view. Recall that managing belief polarization is a matter of keeping ourselves mindful of the range of acceptable doctrinal variation among our allies. We achieve this by seeing the various ways in which our political commitments can be articulated, and exposing our views to reasonable criticism can reveal this. By contrast, the direct clash between our political commitments and the opposition's competing proposals is likely only to inflame polarization. Although engagement of this latter sort is necessary in the broader course of democratic politics, it is counterproductive with respect to polarization management.

The trouble is that in contexts of real-time and face-to-face political engagement, this crucial distinction is too slippery to hold in place. For one thing, we are prone to a particular cognitive error that muddies the distinction. This is the error of inferring from the fact that our opponents hold false and misguided political views that they are also incapable of formulating a decent criticism of our position. We dismiss their criticisms by appeal to our negative assessment of their positive positions; we point to their misguided views as a means of *explaining away* their opposition to ours.

This error is compounded by the fact that when we are embroiled in political discussion, we slide freely from offering our criticisms of our opponent's views to asserting considerations that favor our own position. Our interlocutors naturally do the same. Political argument is notoriously messy in this way, and for that reason it's often frustrating. This messiness is compounded by the fact that interpersonal interactions among political opponents are burdened by escalating negative affect.[32] We tend to see our opponents as untrustworthy and dishonest, and so we have a difficult time hearing their reasons against our position as anything other than brute assertions of their positive views.

Yet if my proposal for sustaining democracy is going to work, we need to be able to separate out reasonable criticisms of our position from the independent considerations that purportedly favor the positive views of our opponents. As this often cannot be done in real-time political interactions among partisan opponents, we need to find a different context for this kind of political thinking. Thus, the second step that we must take: in order to manage belief polarization, we need *distance* from the political fray so that the different kinds of consideration can be sorted and kept distinct.

The idea that we occasionally need to gain distance from our political rifts might sound strange. Some might take it to advocate the kind of democratic disengagement that I rejected earlier. These misgivings arise because we tend to understand political participation as intrinsically public, observable, interpersonal, and collective. When we think of an active and participatory democracy, we envision citizens assembled in public spaces expressing their views. We think of marches, demonstrations, debates, rallies, protests, and such. More generally, we associate political engagement with face-to-face activities that are focused on present problems and decisions. With the intriguing exception of casting votes, we tend to understand citizenship as necessarily nonsolitary.

According to our ordinary conception, then, democracy takes at least two people, and often many more than two, assembled in public. That's why it's noisy. It happens in the streets, so to speak. Take a moment to Google the phrase "what democracy looks like," and you'll see what I mean.

Nevertheless, we readily acknowledge in most other areas of life that there's such a thing as too much togetherness. We understand the need for space, for separateness from others. The concept of "oversharing" is widely recognized, as is the idea that associates can smother each other or be too "clingy." We generally recognize that in order to flourish, our interpersonal relationships need periods of *distance*. Importantly, this distance is not a *relief* from one's relations. It is not a temporary suspension of our associations or an abandoning of our responsibilities to them. It does not involve the assertion of *privacy*, or a kind of *release* from others. Rather, episodes of aloneness positively contribute to one's capacity to be a supportive friend, partner, collaborator, and ally. Occasionally gaining distance is a way of fulfilling our responsibilities to one another.

But when it comes to democratic politics, distance is underrated. In fact, as is indicated by the anecdotes with which this chapter began, it's often treated with suspicion. It's commonly thought that stepping out of publicly observable interaction or refraining from political discussion is *necessarily* a retreat from citizenship as such. However, I have shown in these pages that there's a point where the business of democratic citizenship is undermined by all the collective political hyperactivity. In order to sustain democracy, then, we need to be able to occasionally distance ourselves from the clamor of politics.

To be clear, democracy needs active citizens to engage publicly on behalf of their political convictions. It needs them to be noisy participants in the ongoing contestation of the terms of political association. It needs coalitions to press firmly for greater accountability and social change. But democracy also needs citizens to be reflective and introspective, reserved and thoughtful.

That's not to call for political disengagement.[33] It is rather to affirm that there are important modes of democratic engagement that involve seclusion and contemplation. It is to acknowledge that democracy can happen in libraries and easy chairs as well as in the streets and the corridors of power. Quieter undertakings of political reflection pull us away from the public manifestations of democratic citizenship. Although they might appear to be forms of idleness, they nonetheless are exercises of citizenship. And these exercises require detachment from others and distance from the political fray. As odd as it might sound, in order to sustain democracy, we need *solitude*.

More specifically, if we are to recognize the vulnerability of our political ideas to reasonable criticism and thereby manage belief polarization, we need to secure certain kinds of distance from the throes of politics. The required distance can be usefully described along three closely related dimensions.

First, we need distance from our fellow citizens, opponents and allies alike. Given the affective gears of the polarization dynamic, we need space to discern and grapple with the objections of our reasonable critics. We need space to think through their criticisms, a setting free from the immediate pressure to defend against them. Ideally, these spaces should detach us from our allies as well, lest we fall into the social dynamics that pressure us to conform to the dominant expectations operative within our alliances. This means that although we tend to associate democracy principally with face-to-face and real-time interaction among citizens, we need to remember that in addition to talking and expressing, citizenship calls for *reading* and *thinking*. Importantly, it calls for accessing the opposition's own accounts of the flaws in our views, rather than our own side's expositions of them.

This occasions the need for a second kind of political distance. We also need distance from the criticisms of our *contemporary* opposition. Recall that managing belief polarization is not a matter of weighing our views against the alternatives proposed by our political rivals; it is not a matter of firming up our political resolve in the midst of a coming election or decision. Rather, it has to do with taking steps to acknowledge the ways in which our political views can be reasonably criticized. Yet belief polarization leads us to dismiss and discount the ideas of those we perceive to be our opponents. When we're in the grip of the polarization dynamic, we tend to see an expanding proportion of our opponents as unreasonable and therefore incapable of reasonable criticism. So, we are likely to have difficulty identifying criticisms of our views that strike us as *reasonable*. When confronting this difficulty, we need to turn to critics who are not our fellow citizens, but who nonetheless present reasons against our political positions and orientation. Depending on the circumstance, we might find it helpful to consult writers from prior decades, or even those who are contemporary but writing within the political environment of a democracy different from our own. In short, if we cannot find reasonable criticism among our *present* political opposition, we need to broaden our search to other times and places.

Thus, a third kind of political distance. In placing so much emphasis on the give-and-take of real-time engagement, we have tethered our view of democracy too exclusively to the *politics of the moment*—the problems, debates, struggles, and decisions that confront us today. In a way, this is understandable; self-government is largely about making decisions for a relatively local future, given present circumstances. Yet when this fact of democracy becomes the whole of our conception of political engagement, citizens' political thinking is constrained by the categories, rivalries, and fractures of the moment. Often, these strictures are themselves the orchestrations of national parties and other political formations operating under conditions of political polarization. They thrive because they are able to excite polarized sentiments, motivate political expression, and inflame partisan animosity.

From the first-person perspective, the resulting behavior might *feel like* earnest and civil political engagement with our opposition, but in fact it is mostly choreographed for us and designed to solidify further our partisan identities. Although these Manichean scripts may help to focus attention and stimulate action regarding the issues at hand, they give us no sense of a future where existing forms of partisanship might be overcome and replaced by alternative political categories. In our fixation on winning the current battles, we lose sight of the possibility of a kind of political progress where we have not only *defeated* our opposition, but also *changed* them, thus remaking our rivalries. In this sense, the politics of the moment simply *is* the politics of the polarization dynamic.

Recall the interactions described at the start of this chapter. Operative in many of those encounters was the insistence that political discussion *necessitated* an explicit verdict about the latest campaign episode, as if such judgments were the *currency* with which political exchange must be conducted. No interlocutor understood my "I'm still thinking" remark to be *itself* a kind of political stance. None of them took me to be expressing the judgment that the significance of the event in question wouldn't be clear until the candidates had had a chance to react to it. Again, the idea that political verdicts can take time, or that under certain circumstances one needs to wait for additional information, had been abandoned. The prevailing view contends that to realize what has happened is to know what to think.

The politics of the moment is hence the politics of the insta-verdict, the unblinking judgment, and the hot take. It is thus also the politics of overconfidence and intellectual arrogance. It is democracy for know-it-alls who take reflection to be political irresolution and thus partisan inauthenticity.[34] Yet when democratic engagement is seen in this way, only familiar and commonplace ideas and sentiments are legible as properly political. Citizens simply recite inherited partisan scripts. The result is that political interactions become nothing more than performances of partisanship, authenticity rituals enacted for our political allies.

If we are to sustain democracy, then, we need to gain distance from the politics of the moment. We need occasionally to depart from the prevailing circumstances, the pressing problems and questions, and the partisan battles that compose the immediate political environment. Put positively, we need to acknowledge that democratic citizenship requires us sometimes to think large thoughts, to speculate in ways that are divorced from the urgencies of our immediate political circumstances, to conceive of political futures that are unlikely or even utopian, but which nonetheless reflect a more complete realization of the democratic aspiration. In short, if we are to manage belief polarization, we need sometimes to envision circumstances where our present modes of partisanship have been displaced, not because partisanship and its related animosities are eliminable from democracy, but because our present rivalries and divides are, in the end, products of contingency and thus always in flux.

To repeat, in stressing the need for political distance, I have not been calling for a withdrawal from politics. The point rather has been that although political distance involves separating from what I have called the *fray* of democratic politics, it is not a form of political disengagement. Taking the necessary distancing measures is *itself* an act of citizenship. It is aimed at sustaining democracy. Moreover, my case for the necessity of political distance does not deny that citizens *also* need to enter the fray of current politics and take part in the usual kinds of public democratic action. The proposal instead is that *in addition to* public and interpersonal political engagement, democratic citizens also need to perform acts of distanced political reflection and imagination. Indeed, my argument has been that in the absence of occasions for distanced contemplation, the public and interpersonal forms of democratic participation are self-undermining. If we want to serve democracy, we sometimes need to take our politics off the streets, away from the glow of our screens, and out of one another's face.

## 4.  Conclusion

The central argument of this book is now complete. It can be summarized succinctly. The challenge of sustaining democracy can be captured in two questions: *Why should we?* and *How can we?* In response to the first question, the argument has been that we should sustain democracy with our foes because our political alliances and objectives depend on it. In reply to the second, I have argued that we can sustain democracy by taking steps to manage belief polarization within ourselves and among our allies.

Let's review these in order. The democrat's dilemma emerges from a conflict between two central directives of citizenship. On the one hand, we are partners in self-government and must take responsibility for our politics. This means not only that we are duty bound to participate in the joint undertakings of democracy, but also that we must seek to enact justice and a fuller realization of the democratic aspiration. In this sense, we must allow politics to get into our heads, to some extent—we must take up the office of citizenship. As democracy is self-government among equals, we must embody the virtue of civility in our political engagements. That is, we must endeavor to exercise our political judgment in ways that are informed by the perspectives, ideas, concerns, and criticism of our fellow citizens. Yet, on the other hand, ordinary political interaction places us in contact with fellow citizens who embrace political ideas that strike us as misguided, unwarranted, counterproductive, and perhaps inconsistent with justice. Sometimes, our opponents strike us as only marginally committed to democracy. Hence the dilemma: why strive to uphold civility in our relations with those who promote political ideas that are out of step with justice and who in any case seem to us to be divested from the democratic aspiration? As I have stressed throughout, we must note that this dilemma emerges out of sincere and otherwise laudable democratic citizenship.

*Why should we* sustain democracy when the stakes are high and our opponents strike us as democratically delinquent? The answer relies on an examination of political and belief polarization, and the resulting dynamic between them. Put simply, these phenomena lead us to *over-ascribe* extreme commitments and malignant attitudes to those whom we perceive to be relevantly unlike ourselves. Thus, as partisan identity has captured the center of our overall sense of ourselves, we have grown more inclined to embrace distorted conceptions of our partisan opponents that lead us to see them as uncivil, unreasonable, and divested from democracy. The challenge of sustaining democracy is in part a matter of correcting for these distortions.

Yet the answer to the *"why should we"* question is ultimately not about our opponents at all. My argument has *not* been that we should sustain democracy because our opponents are owed our civility. To be clear, provided that our opponents are reasonable, they indeed are owed civility. However, I have argued that a central reason we should sustain democracy with our opposition has to do with our allies and coalitions. When we elect to *suspend* democracy with our foes, the forces of the polarization dynamic turn within, escalating the demands for conformity within our alliances. As these demands intensify and expand, our coalitions both fracture and become increasingly hierarchical. Both of these outcomes are debilitating for our political objectives. Recall that our fervor for serving the interests of justice is what drives the democrat's dilemma in the first place. Thus, my response to the dilemma: We have moral reasons to preserve our ability to act politically in ways that promote justice and further the democratic aspiration. Therefore, we have a moral reason to sustain democracy with our opponents even when the stakes are high and when we suspect they are not fully invested in the democratic project.

Of course, this is not to say that we are required to sustain democracy at all costs, even after our opposition has proven to be unreasonable. Civility is not a unilateral requirement. Correcting for our tendency to over-ascribe broadly unreasonable traits to our opponents shouldn't be met with an *overcorrection* that naively proceeds as if all of our political foes are indeed staunch democrats whom we simply have misunderstood. No—some citizens are indeed unreasonable, uninterested in civility, and divested from the democratic aspiration. They must be dealt with in some way.

However, the question of how to politically engage with unreasonable citizens is different from the one we have been investigating. We have developed an account of how democratic citizens should proceed given that earnest political engagement exposes them to forces that provoke the democrat's dilemma and hence lead them to over-ascribe incivility to their opponents. If the response is simply that we should suspend democracy whenever we *suspect* or even *sincerely believe* that our opposition has divested from the democratic ethos, we embrace the idea that self-government among equals is possible only among citizens who agree about politics. But that's to say that democracy is not really possible. It's to concede that democracy is never anything other than a cold civil war.

Still, I have affirmed that democracy *is* a kind of political struggle among opponents. What sets democracy apart from being a cold civil war is that the opponents must regard one another as political equals, each entitled to an equal say. The difficulty lies in the fact that the political activities that are proper for democratic participants heighten citizens' exposure to forces that erode their capacity to recognize their opponents' equality. So, if we seek to sustain democracy, we need to work on ourselves. We need to find ways to manage belief polarization within ourselves and our alliances. The hope is that in taking steps to manage belief polarization, citizens will be in a better position to accurately draw the distinction between their severely misguided but nonetheless reasonable political opposition and those who are truly beyond the pale of the democratic ideal. The crucial thing, however, is that although belief polarization is driven by strained relations between political opponents, the task of managing it lies within. Our second question thus emerges.

*How can we* sustain democracy? What steps can we take to manage belief polarization? I have laid out a two-step proposal. First, we can manage belief polarization within ourselves by establishing practices and habits that keep us mindful of the vulnerability of our political views to reasonable criticism. This calls us to seek out and engage with the ideas of our reasonable critics. Importantly, the idea is *not* that we must strive to appreciate the merits of the other side's views. It is rather to grapple with the limitations of our own views by taking steps to acknowledge that our political ideas are *improvable* by means of reasonable criticism. The hope is that by exposing our commitments to reasonable criticism, we can loosen the doctrinal constrictions that emerge within our thinking and within alliances without thereby putting our political identity under threat.

Second, we must supplement our public political engagement with occasions of political reflection by creating forms of distance from the fray of partisan politics. We must make space for political reflection, imagination, and self-examination. We need to reckon honestly with the improvability of our political ideas. This means that, insofar as it is possible, these activities must be engaged outside of the presence of our political foes and allies. We need to unglue ourselves, not from democratic politics, but from the orchestrations and curations of those who benefit from the partisan status quo. That is to say that this space must be free from the encroachments of the politics of the moment.

Under certain favorable conditions these steps might yield broader democratic benefits. For example, successful belief polarization management might improve citizens' political opinions, make for more productive political disagreements, and repair fractures among opposed partisans. Still, I have emphasized that these measures aim strictly at managing belief polarization, not at other kinds of democratic improvement. Sustaining democracy is not sufficient for creating a flourishing society of self-governing equals. It is only necessary.

All in all, I have shown that even though the democrat's dilemma arises out of political activity of the familiar public and interpersonal kind, the task of citizenship also involves quieter and more solitary pursuits. We typically think of democratic citizenship strictly in terms of its external manifestations: discussing, debating, canvassing, voting, rallying, demonstrating, and so on. That's part of the problem. Democracy of course involves all of these activities. But sustaining democracy begins at home. What we owe to the other side is to sustain democracy on our own side. And this requires us to cultivate democracy within ourselves.

# Epilogue

## Living Together as Equals

Just as I finished writing the previous chapter, I came across the following story in my social media timeline:

> *Since going into lockdown, the only daily socializing I do outside of the house is walking my dog with my sexagenarian, rural Massachusetts neighbors. We are not politically aligned, I did not expect this relationship. But we have become quite close.*
>
> *We know that our politics don't agree, and sometimes Mark will make a teasing joke we both know is predicated on sincere disagreement. But mostly our relationship is about taking care of each other: cooking, chores, shopping, dog baths, and general pet care.*
>
> *Yesterday they invited us for Thanksgiving dinner. We'll be in DC with Steve's folks, so we had to decline. They immediately insisted they will take Milo while we are out of town, because it will be better for the dogs to be together than to have a babysitter.*
>
> *But here's another thing: on a walk a few weeks ago, Mark asked me to "answer a question for an old redneck." He asked about the inclusion of "Q" in LGBTQ. "Does it really mean 'queer'???" He said that for him, that word was a slur, and he felt uncomfortable saying it out loud.*
>
> *We had a good, sincere conversation. Again, this person thinks my politics are bananas. He supports policies and politicians that I generally think of as beyond the pale. And yet.*

This story was posted by the philosopher Lauren Leydon-Hardy, as part of a casual thread discussing themes related to my book *Overdoing Democracy*. I share it here with her permission. It captures nicely the central argument of that work: we need to navigate our partisan differences against a backdrop of nonpolitical activities and relationships. Here, two neighbors had established a social relationship on basis of dog-walking and neighborliness. This allowed them to engage their political differences in ways that manifest their mutual recognition of each other's political equality. Although they remain sharply divided politically, this opposition is accompanied by a broader horizon of shared values and ideals in which politics is simply not the point. *Overdoing Democracy* argues that if we seek to perform well as democratic citizens, we need sometimes to engage together in cooperative activities in which politics is not so much suppressed or bracketed, but rather has no place at all.

Lauren's story has something to teach us about sustaining democracy, too. Mark asked for help in *better understanding* something. He did not seek to initiate an argument about the politics of sex and gender terminology, but rather expressed interest in better informing his view by listening to what a reasonable critic might say about it. What's more, he prefaced his question with an explicit recognition that his perspective is a manifestation of his broader social identity—he acknowledged that he was thinking about the matter from a particular position, that of an "old redneck." In this way, he had taken steps for managing belief polarization of the kind that were recommended in Chapter 4.

The ensuing conversation was "sincere." They did not come to an agreement. It's likely that no one's mind was changed. In that sense, Lauren and Mark still see each other as political rivals. Yet each furthered their own understanding of how the opposition sees their position. Pursuing this kind of political self-awareness marks a crucial first step in breaking the polarization dynamic. I must confess that before reading this story, I had never considered the possibility that conservative resistance to inclusivist gender language could be driven by the concern that words like "queer" are slurs. It is far more common for this resistance to be perceived as the manifestation of brute prejudice. In any case, Lauren and Mark are likely to continue regarding each other as politically misguided, but neither can see the other as wholly depraved and unfit for democracy. They can live together as equals.

There's hope for democracy yet. Still, democracy is rooted in a handful of hard truths about politics. First among these is that you can't always get what you want. In fact, you often can't avoid getting what you don't want. Knowing the truth about what justice requires, what government ought to do, or which candidate is best does not entitle you to get your way. Nor does your ability to dismantle the arguments of your opponents or to expose their intellectual flaws. Thus, a harder political truth: you can't always get what you know is right.

There's more. Despite your knowledge of important political matters and your ability to refute your foes, when your side loses at the polls, it would be illegitimate for government to enact your will rather than theirs. For electoral losers the principal consolation is that there'll be another election at some point down the road, and thus another chance to try to get one's fellow citizens to see the light. Of course, this means that in the wake of an electoral defeat, those who care about justice must redouble their political efforts. Knowing what's right in politics makes for more work, not less.

Political defeat can be exhausting. Yet, in a democracy, political victory is also difficult. Even when you do get what you want, and even when justice prevails, you *still* can't have it all. Your political rivals retain their status as equal citizens even when they're demonstrably in the wrong. Losing at the polls does not mean that the opposition must acquiesce. They're entitled to object, criticize, resist, complain, and campaign on behalf of what you regard as injustice. Moreover, even when our opponents are politically impaired and democratically disingenuous, it remains true that politics is a matter of exercising power among political equals. Even when justice prevails at the polls, political power must be justifiable to the citizens over whom it is exercised, even when they embrace flawed and perverse political opinions. Democratic government thus is required not merely to *allow* electoral losers to continue pressing their opposition. It must *provide* them a platform for their advocacy, even when they're in the wrong. Here's the hardest of the hard truths: democracy *empowers* justice and injustice alike.

That's a lot to take in. Democracy's critics say that it's simply too much. One way we can resign ourselves to these hard truths is by tacitly adopting a view commonly attributed to Winston Churchill: whatever its flaws, democracy is the best kind of society given the available alternatives. This provides an understandable degree of comfort—democracy is indeed the best among our options. But seeing democracy in this way sells it short. Churchill concedes that democracy can be nothing more than the succession of various politicians dominating one another in turn, according to rules designed to keep peace. It implicitly accepts the idea of democracy as a cold civil war.

Once we embrace the idea that democracy is a cold civil war, we might as well ask ourselves why we shouldn't turn up the heat, especially if our side has the upper hand. We come to reason that politics is fickle, and when the power shifts in favor of the other side, they can't be trusted to uphold the terms of our détente. It seems to us that if given the chance, *they'd* seek to end the cold civil war by imposing an unconditional surrender. Why not escalate while we have the power? That's the problem with cold civil wars. Even though they're cold, they're volatile.

In this book I have presented an alternative picture of democracy rooted in the idea of political equality. Although democracy often proceeds by a kind of combat, we keep the temperature low by acknowledging that beneath it all, we remain one another's equals. Thus, as democratic citizens, we must recognize that our adversaries do not merely *get* an equal say in politics; they're *entitled* to one. And even when their political opinions are odious and their judgment is flawed, democracy involves the recognition that there is a fundamental indignity in being merely *subject* to political power, responsible for compliance with rules that one has no say in crafting. Accordingly, democracy aspires for a society in which exercises of political power are consistent with the dignity of those who are subjected to them. It is the proposition that *in spite of* ongoing deep disputes about how political power should be deployed, citizens can serve as equal partners in the collective task of self-government.

In short, democracy is the proposal that indeed we can live together as equals. As inspiring as this idea might be, this book has shown that essential modes of democratic participation can cause responsible citizens to betray it. Recall that in order to have an effective democratic voice, we typically need to join a chorus. So, as we advocate sincerely on behalf of our political commitments, partisan attachment gets inside our heads. We thereby expose ourselves to social and cognitive forces that inhibit our capacity to recognize political opponents as our equals. We eventually give up on the democratic aspiration.

We owe it to one another to uphold this aspiration. That's easier said than done. In a democracy, political division is unavoidable. Living together as equals thus means living with others whose politics we reject and might even despise. It also means recognizing that some of our fellow citizens are reasonable, despite their misguided opinions. Hence, we owe it to the other side—specifically, our reasonable adversaries—to sustain in ourselves and among our allies the attitudes and dispositions that make us capable of proper citizenship. Most generally, we owe it to them to cultivate within ourselves the virtue of civility.

Democracy in the United States is captured by the polarization dynamic. Our thinking is slotted into the categories that the dynamic itself has manufactured. We thus incline too strongly to

ascribe uncivil traits and tendencies to our opponents. We tend
to see them as uniformly divested from the democratic ethos.
Although political engagement feels like authentic expression of
our deepest moral commitments, it is largely scripted for us. It thus
is destined to maintain the partisan status quo. We cannot cultivate civility by focusing directly on repairing relations with our
adversaries. Instead, we must look inward—to ourselves and our
political alliances—and adopt strategies for managing belief polarization within. I have argued that in order to do this we first must
create occasions for encountering reasonable criticisms of our
views. This enables one to stay mindful of the fact that one's position is improvable, and thus that there is a spectrum of reasonable doctrinal variation among one's allies. As odd as it may sound,
what we owe to the other side is to be a responsible advocate for our
own. Responsible advocacy requires self-criticism. Self-criticism is
risky. Not only can it lead us to reassess our ideas and thus who we
are, but it can also strain our political alliances. This suggests that
sustaining democracy involves an additional virtue: courage.

The bulk of this book was completed in the days following the
2020 presidential election in the United States, just as the election
returns showed conclusively that Joe Biden would be the 46th president. For many, this result came as an enormous relief, a sign of
a brighter future for the country. For many who support Donald
Trump, however, the outcome posed a threat, an abandoning of
democracy. After obscenely declaring victory on the evening of
Election Day, Donald Trump pledged to contest the outcome immediately after returns showed a solid popular and electoral victory for Biden. In the weeks following Election Day, Trump and
his team repeatedly asserted without evidence that the election
somehow had been rigged in favor of Biden. Baseless lawsuits
were filed, and eventually dismissed. A large-scale disinformation campaign was launched alleging widespread voter fraud,
rigged voting machines, discarded ballots, and other forms of sab-
otage. Republican Party leadership contributed in various ways,

sometimes directly asserting that the election was indeed fraudulent, other times simply declining to affirm that Biden had indeed
won the election. In the weeks following Election Day, belief that
the allegations of electoral fraud were true was widespread among
Trump's supporters.

Then came January 6, the day that members of the Senate and the
House of Representatives meet with the vice president to officially
ratify the states' Electoral College votes. A mob that had gathered
for a "Save America" rally was prompted by Donald Trump and
others to "fight like hell" for the country; they took up the call and
stormed the US Capitol. I watched in frozen horror. A Canadian
journalist called me to ask simply, "What's happening?" My reply
was understandably scattered: "The vice president's life is in danger.
Nancy Pelosi's life is in danger. Some of them are carrying zip ties.
They're planning to take hostages. Where are the police? No one's
being arrested. I can't believe what I'm seeing."

As I write this, a month has passed since that day. New footage of
the episode routinely emerges. At least one civilian and three police
officers lost their lives due to these events. Hundreds were injured
and traumatized. I still can't fully process what transpired, except
to say that groups of far-right insurrectionists, white supremacists,
and nationalists were mixed together with more run-of-the-mill
Trump devotees who had bought into the lies about voter fraud
and other conspiracies. The combination was volatile. Provocation
from Trump himself was all that was needed to set lawlessness in
motion. Trump has since been impeached for inciting violence
against the government.

As things stand, it is unlikely that the Senate will vote to con-
vict. In fact, the majority of Republican lawmakers are on record
*opposing* the impeachment and the coming trial. One main argument is that an impeachment trial will be too divisive for a country
that is already so deeply divided. Better to turn the page and allow
the country to heal, many Republicans have said. Of course,
the counterargument is that there could be no healing without

responsibility. The argument runs that the way to repair divisions is to uphold our legal and moral norms, and this requires us to hold those who attacked our democracy accountable. Meanwhile, some of the forces that fomented the distrust, resentment, and rage that led to the riot at the Capitol have regrouped and begun calling for further action of that kind. It's a precarious time.

This book is not addressed to these grim circumstances. However, it explains some of the factors that brought us to them. When we allow politics to get inside our heads but then do not take steps to manage belief polarization, we become unable to see our opposition as anything other than a unified monolith of extremity and unreasonableness. Thus, when we lose at the polls, it feels as if democracy itself has been defeated. When these attitudes are combined with potent forms of encouragement from our allies, we come to see any election in which our side does not prevail as fraudulent. We find ourselves embracing the contradictory view that democracy is proper only when it delivers the results we favor.

Of course, our most fervent opponents see us in a similar light. Hence incivility, distrust, and animosity escalate. Each side eventually suspends democratic relations with the other, thereby adopting the stance that democracy is possible only when the other side is dominated and shut down. This stance causes the debilitating forces of the polarization dynamic to turn within and corrode democracy among allies. In the end, democracy loses.

This book points to a task before us. Assuming for the moment, hopefully, that the worst can be averted in the wake of the US election, there remains the challenge of rebuilding trust in democracy. This obviously must involve a change in tone among the political leadership. Thinking of politics in general, and the presidency in particular, as an exercise of domination over one's partisan rivals is potent rhetoric, but it's toxic for democracy. For four years, the United States coped with an administration that explicitly regarded political power as something to be wielded for the purpose of its own enlargement. That this view has become predominant in the name of conservatism is one of the deep ironies of modern politics. In any case, the new leadership must amplify its commitment to fundamentally democratic values, especially the principle that citizens are never merely subjects of the government's rule, even when they affiliate with the party that does not hold power. The impulse to do otherwise, to use political power strictly to deracinate the Republican Party, is strong. Many will insist on it. Indeed, many will see anything less than this as an irrational concession to an already wounded foe. This stance ensures that the polarization dynamic remains firmly in place.

The alternative I have proposed does not require political reconciliation. I have not argued that political victors must appease the other side or meet them halfway. We need not love our political enemies. The prescription rather is that those who hold power must wield it responsibly, with due recognition of the fact that those over whom it is exercised remain political equals. We thus are called to formulate our political positions in ways that show regard for the perspectives and concerns of reasonable opponents. This does not require us to modify or relax our views. Rather, it asks officeholders and citizens to fortify the rationales they can provide in support of them.

Still, the way forward does not lie strictly with leaders. The pathologies of the polarization dynamic flow in multiple directions. The packaging and marketing of candidates, along with the governing style and public demeanor of those who win office, are determined by strategic calculations about the character of the citizenry. In a 2017 speech, Barack Obama said that a society gets the politicians it deserves. It is more accurate to say that we get the politicians we ask for.

A deeply polarized citizenry makes the job of political strategists and campaign managers all too easy. Polarization also calcifies the status quo, preserving circumstances where citizens are submerged in their preassigned partisan roles and thus stuck with their animosities and resentments. The rehabilitation of democracy thus does not lie exclusively with politicians and parties. They are the *beneficiaries* of the status quo. Sustaining democracy is the challenge of reorienting our relationships with our political commitments in light of our vulnerability to belief polarization. This in turn requires us to remake our alliances so that they do not feed the polarization dynamic. In this sense, the democratic task before us lies within. Living together as equals is up to us.

# Notes

## Introduction

1. Back in 2017, the progressive philosopher Cornel West and conservative legal theorist Robert P. George jointly authored a statement affirming their shared conception of "truth seeking, democracy, and freedom of thought and expression," which captures this common ground nicely.
2. Pew Research Center 2016.
3. See the study The Perception Gap and the accompanying interactive website, (https://perceptiongap.us/). See also Mounk 2019.
4. Pew Research Center 2014.

## Chapter 1

1. See, for example, Landemore 2020; Mulligan 2018; Guerrero 2014; and López-Guerra 2011.
2. Some democratic theorists would depart from this tenet. However, they argue that certain systems that deviate from full and equal suffrage tend to *better realize* the underlying ideal of popular rule. See Estlund 2000; and, again, Landemore 2020; Mulligan 2018; Guerrero 2014; and López-Guerra 2011.
3. Pettit 2012: 84ff.
4. Citizens in the United States tend to *vote* in ways that are public-spirited in this sense—they are strongly disinclined to vote strictly on the basis of what they perceive to be their narrow self-interest. See Funk 2000.

## Chapter 2

1. Pew Research Center 2019a.
2. Margalit 2010: 19f.
3. It bears repeating here that my claim is *not* that citizens adopt large-scale theories of justice and then infer from them their opinions in specific cases.

No doubt the average citizen's political thinking is far more complicated. The point instead is that when we formulate an opinion about a specific issue, we *take ourselves* to be inferring it from our broader political stance.

4. Margolis 2018; Margolis 2016.

5. Mason and Wronski 2018.

6. Mason 2018a; Iyengar 2016.

7. Rawls 2005: 58ff. In my opinion, Rawls's term carries certain intuitive resonances. However, it is also tied to difficulties with Rawls's larger view. I am using the term in a way that does not raise these difficulties.

8. Here we encounter a limitation of the Rawlsian term. In the vernacular, "reasonable" is frequently used to assign to an idea some degree of plausibility, some likelihood of being true. The Rawlsian stipulation, which we are following, does not carry this connotation.

9. This assessment comes in varying strengths. Imaging yourself holding with respect to some political issue that the status quo is proper. You are thus bound to see anyone calling for change as mistaken, advocating for a departure from what is just. Of course, the views of those who embrace more modest deviations will strike you as preferable to the views of those seeking more sweeping changes. But, as you hold that the status quo is proper, anyone pursuing change is for that reason in the wrong. Next imagine a different case where you advocate change from the status quo. Obviously, those who seek to maintain the status quo will strike you as on the side of injustice. But so, too, will those calling for changes from the status quo that differ from those you support. Some will want a less dramatic change than what you advocate, while others will press for changes that go beyond what you think is warranted, and so on. In these cases, we might see our opposition as falling short or going beyond justice—or, as I put it earlier, *missing the mark*. Still, in any of these cases, there will be others who promote views that will strike you as *moving in the wrong direction* from the status quo. Depending on the details, you might assess these views as what I've called *setbacks*. But in more severe cases, one might see a setback as a positive *affront* to justice.

## Chapter 3

1. Ultimately, I'm not sure that this is a more generous way of stating the diagnosis, as it is aimed at casting opponents as pitiable rather than contemptable. Arguably, the former is more insulting.

2. This is known as the "black sheep effect." See Marques, Yzerbyt, and Leyens 1988.
3. Klein 2020: xix.
4. This section and the next condense and revise the account I give of polarization in Chapter 4 of *Overdoing Democracy* (Talisse 2019).
5. In the United States, the terms "RINO" (Republican in name only) and "DINO" (Democrat in name only) serve this purpose.
6. This is often called *affective* polarization, but for reasons that will become clear in the next section, this term is misleading in the present context. See Iyengar et al. 2019 for a review.
7. Levendusky and Malhorta 2016.
8. Iyengar and Krupenkin 2018; Mason 2018b.
9. Iyengar, Sood, and Lelkes 2012.
10. McConnell et al. 2017; Hetherington and Weiler 2018; Mason 2018a.
11. Iyengar and Westwood 2015: 691f.
12. Huber and Malhotra 2017; Iyengar and Konitzer 2017.
13. Mason 2018a: 14.
14. Bougher 2017.
15. Beyond Conflict 2020.
16. Ahler 2014; Alher and Sood 2018.
17. Lee 2016.
18. Iyengar and Krupenkin 2018: 215.
19. See Tosi and Warmke 2020: ch. 7 for discussion of political grandstanding.
20. Pew Research Center 2019b.
21. It is worth noting here that what I am calling "belief polarization" is generally called "group polarization" in the professional literature. In the present context, however, this more common name is misleading. I am trying to keep political polarization and belief polarization distinct, and both phenomena have to do with groups. Calling one "group polarization" would, I think, invite unclarity.
22. Westfall et al. 2015; Sunstein 2009: 44.
23. Hence Lamm and Myers (1978: 146): "Seldom in the history of social psychology has a nonobvious phenomenon been so firmly grounded in data from across a variety of cultures and dependent measures."
24. The appendix in Sunstein 2009 provides summaries of the most important experimental findings.
25. Moscovici and Zavalloni 1969.
26. Myers and Bishop 1970: 778–779.
27. Myers 1975.

28. Hastie, Schkade, and Sunstein 2007; Sunstein 2009: 5–8.

29. The phenomenon known as "risky shift," where a group's post-discussion likeliness to engage in risky collective behavior exceeds any of its individual members' pre-discussion willingness to endorse that level of risk for the group, is frequently understood to be a special case of belief polarization. See Isenberg 1986: 1141.

30. Schkade, Sunstein, and Kahneman 2000.

31. Johnson, Stemler, and Hunter 1977.

32. Turner et al. 1987: 153.

33. Baron et al. 1996: 548.

34. Turner et al. 1987: 153.

35. Sia, Tan, and Wei 2002: 71–72.

36. Abrams et al. 1990.

37. Lord, Ross, and Lepper 1979.

38. Sunstein 2009: 33; Myers et al. 1980.

39. Lamm and Myers 1978.

40. Baron et al. 1996.

41. Hogg 2001.

42. Baron et al. 1996: 558–559.

43. Keating, Van Boven, and Judd 2016.

44. Baron et al. 1996: 559.

45. Mason 2018a: 14; Mason 2015; Iyengar and Westwood 2015.

46. Bishop 2009: 40; Chen and Rodden 2013; Tam Cho, Gimpel, and Hui 2013.

47. Pew Research Center 2019a.

48. Nyhan and Reifler 2010.

49. Puglisi and Snyder 2011; Sood and Iyengar 2016.

50. Hogg 2001.

51. Jaggers 2019.

52. Marques, Yzerbyt, and Leyens 1988.

53. Iyengar and Krupenkin 2018.

# Chapter 4

1. Pew Research Center 2019b.

2. Kahan et al. 2012.

3. Iyengar and Westwood 2015; Hetherington and Weiler 2018.

4. Claassen and Ensley 2016.

5. Munro, Weih, and Tsai 2010.

6. Marks et al. 2018.
7. Nyhan and Reifler 2010.
8. Bail et al. 2018.
9. Talisse 2019: ch. 3.
10. Mason 2018a; Iyengar and Westwood 2015.
11. George Lakoff (2002) has advanced a similar thesis according to which it lies within the nature of cognition that persons who hold different values see the world in different—conflicting and irreconcilable—ways. My claim here is more modest, as it identifies the source of these differences within the depth of partisan identity, not cognition as such. See also Hetherington and Weiler 2018: 10–21.
12. Indeed, our judgments about what behavior should count as hypocritical track our partisan affiliations. See Weston et al. 2006.
13. Achen and Bartels 2016: 276ff. See also Kahan et al. 2012; and Iyengar et al. 2019: 136–139.
14. Orwell (1946) 1968: 125.
15. See Neblo et al. 2010; Steiner 2012; and the essays collected in Parkinson and Mansbridge 2012.
16. See Curato et al. 2017 for a summary.
17. See Mansbridge 2010.
18. Goodin 2017.
19. Neblo et al. 2010; Christensen, Himmelroos, and Grönlund 2016.
20. See Mendelberg 2002 for a sobering review of the empirical findings as of 2002.
21. Mutz 2006.
22. Hastie, Schkade, and Sunstein 2007.
23. Bail et al. 2018; Achen and Bartels 2016: 297–303.
24. Sunstein 2017: 91.
25. Curato et al. (2017: 33) claim that "deliberation is the solution" to belief polarization, but then provide documentation showing only that in their experiments, polarization "was not found." Fishkin (2018: 77–78) seems to make a similar error.
26. Fishkin 2018.
27. Stanley et al. 2020.
28. This does not entail that democracy does not need *moderates* or, for that matter, people who think their opposition might, on certain questions, be correct. These both are stances that one can be convinced of. The point is rather that our account of democracy must recognize that staunch political conviction is consistent with proper citizenship.

29. The issue of how to deal with *unreasonable* criticism is intriguing, but outside the scope of the present argument.
30. Mill (1859) 2015: 37.
31. They might be distinct in a deeper sense as well. Snedegar (2018) argues that reasons for are different in *kind* from reasons against.
32. It is noteworthy that the de-escalation studies conducted by Stanley et al. (2020) do not involve interpersonal interactions among political opponents. They find that negative affect eases among partisans when they are exposed to the other side's *reasons*, outside of actual person-to-person engagement.
33. Citizens might need to occasionally withdraw, together, from politics. This is the overarching theme of Talisse 2019.
34. Lynch 2019.

# Works Cited

Abrams, D., M. Wetherell, S. Cochrane, M. A. Hogg, and J. C. Turner. 1990. "Knowing What to Think by Knowing Who You Are: Self-Categorization and the Nature of Norm Formation, Conformity and Group Polarization." *British Journal of Social Psychology* 29.2: 97–119.

Achen, Christopher H., and Larry M. Bartels. 2016. *Democracy for Realists: Why Elections Do Not Produce Responsive Government.* Princeton: Princeton University Press.

Ahler, Douglas J. 2014. "Self-Fulfilling Misperceptions of Public Polarization." *Journal of Politics* 76: 607–620.

Ahler, Douglas J., and Guarav Sood. 2018. "The Parties in Our Heads: Misperception About Party Composition and their Consequences." *Journal of Politics* 80: 964–981.

Bail, Christopher A., Lisa P. Argyle, Taylor W. Brown, John P. Bumpus, Haohan Chen, M. B. Fallin Hunzaker, Jaemin Lee, Marcus Mann, Friedolin Merhout, and Alexander Volfovsky. 2018. "Exposure to Opposing Views on Social Media Can Increase Political Polarization." *Proceedings of the National Academy of Sciences* 115.37: 9216–9221.

Baron, Robert S., Sieg I. Hoppe, Chaun Feng Kao, Bethany Brunsman, Barbara Linneweh, and Diana Rogers. 1996. "Social Corroboration and Opinion Extremity." *Journal of Experimental Social Psychology* 32: 537–560.

Beyond Conflict. 2020. America's Divided Mind. https://beyondconflictint.org/americas-divided-mind/.

Bishop, Bill. 2009. *The Big Sort: Why the Clustering of Like-minded America is Tearing Us Apart.* Boston, MA: Mariner Books.

Bougher, Lori D. 2017. "The Correlates of Discord: Identity, Issue Alignment, and Political Hostility in Polarized America." *Political Behavior* 39: 731–762.

Chen, Jowei, and Jonathan Rodden. 2013, "Unintentional Gerrymandering: Political Geography and Electoral Bias in Legislatures." *Quarterly Journal of Political Science* 8: 239–269.

Christensen, Henrik Serup, Staffan Himmelroos, and Kimmo Grönlund. 2016. "Does Deliberation Breed an Appetite for Discursive Participation? Assessing the Impact of First-Hand Experience." *Political Studies* 65: 64–83.

Claassen, Ryan L., and Michael Ensley. 2016. "Motivated Reasoning and Yard-Sign Stealing Partisans: Mine Is a Likeable Rogue, Yours Is a Degenerate Criminal." *Political Behavior* 38: 317–335.

Curato, Nicole, John S. Dryzek, Selen A. Ercan, Carolyn M. Hendricks, and Simon Niemeyer. 2017. "Twelve Key Findings in Deliberative Democracy Research." *Daedalus*, Summer: 28–38.

Estlund, David. 2000. "Political Quality." *Social Philosophy and Policy* 17: 127–160.

Fishkin, James S. 2018. *Democracy When the People Are Thinking*. New York: Oxford University Press.

Funk, Carolyn L. 2000. "The Dual Influence of Self-Interest and Societal Interest in Public Opinion." *Political Research Quarterly* 53: 37–62.

George, Robert P., and Cornel West. 2017. "Truth Seeking, Democracy, and Freedom of Thought and Expression." https://jmp.princeton.edu/statement.

Goodin, Robert. 2017. "The Epistemic Benefits of Deliberative Democracy." *Policy Sciences* 50: 351–366.

Guerrero, Alexander. 2014. "Against Elections: The Lottocratic Alternative." *Philosophy and Public Affairs* 42: 135–178.

Hastie, Reid, David Schkade, and Cass R. Sunstein. 2007. "What Happened on Deliberation Day?" *California Law Review* 95: 915–940.

Hetherington, Marc, and Jonathan Weiler. 2018. *Prius or Pickup?* Boston: Houghton Mifflin Harcourt.

Hogg, Michael A. 2001. "A Social Identity Theory of Leadership." *Personality and Social Psychology Review* 5: 184–200.

Huber, Gregory A., and Neil Malhotra. 2017. "Political Homophily in Social Relationships: Evidence from Online Dating Behavior." *Journal of Politics* 79: 269–283.

Isenberg, Daniel J. 1986. "Group Polarization: A Critical Review and Meta-Analysis." *Journal of Personality and Social Psychology* 50: 1141–1151.

Iyengar, Shanto. 2016. "*E Pluribus Pluribus*, or Divided We Stand." *Public Opinion Quarterly* 80: 219–224.

Iyengar, Shanto, and Tobias Konitzer. 2017. "The Moderating Effects of Marriage Across Party Lines." Unpublished working paper. https://pdfs.semanticscholar.org/a55b/50f3de44529ee301c662aa42fb244e4ab992.pdf.

Iyengar, Shanto, and Masha Krupenkin. 2018. "The Strengthening of Partisan Affect." *Advances in Political Psychology* 39: 201–218.

Iyengar, Shanto, Yphtach Lelkes, Matthew Levendusky, Neil Malhotra, and Sean J. Westwood. 2019. "The Origins and Consequences of Affective Polarization in the United States." *Annual Review of Political Science* 22: 129–146.

Iyengar, Shanto, Guarav Sood, and Yphach Lelkes. 2012. "Affect, Not Ideology: A Social Identity Perspective on Polarization." *Public Opinion Quarterly* 76: 405–431.

Iyengar, Shanto, and Sean J. Westwood. 2015. "Fear and Loathing Across Party Lines: New Evidence on Group Polarization." *American Journal of Political Science* 59: 690–707.

Jaggers, Zachary. 2019. "Your Political Views Can Predict How You Pronounce Certain Words." *The Conversation.* https://theconversation.com/your-political-views-can-predict-how-you-pronounce-certain-words-124839.

Johnson, Norris R., James G. Stemler, and Deborah Hunter. 1977. "Crowd Behavior as 'Risky Shift': A Laboratory Experiment." *Sociometry* 40: 183–187.

Kahan, Dan M., David A. Hoffman, Donald Braman, Danieli Evans, and Jeffrey J. Rachlinski. 2012. "'They Saw a Protest': Cognitive Illiberalism and the Speech-Conflict Distinction." *Stanford Law Review* 64: 851–906.

Keating, Jessica, Leaf Van Boven, and Charles M. Judd. 2016. "Partisan Underestimation of the Polarizing Influence of Group Discussion." *Journal of Experimental Social Psychology* 65: 52–58.

Klein, Ezra. 2020. *Why We're Polarized.* New York: Avid Reader Press.

Lakoff, George. 2002. *Moral Politics: How Liberals and Conservatives Think.* 2nd edition. Chicago: University of Chicago Press.

Lamm, Helmut, and David Myers. 1978. "Group-Induced Polarization of Attitudes and Behavior." *Advances in Experimental Social Psychology* 11: 145–187.

Landemore, Hélène. 2020. *Open Democracy: Reinventing Popular Rule for the Twenty-First Century.* Princeton: Princeton University Press.

Lee, Frances E. 2016. *Insecure Majorities: Congress and the Perpetual Campaign.* Chicago: University of Chicago Press.

Levendusky, Matthew, and Neil Malhorta. 2016. "Does Media Coverage of Partisan Polarization Affect Political Attitudes?" *Political Communication* 33: 283–301.

López-Guerra, Claudio. 2011. "The Enfranchisement Lottery." *Philosophy, Politics, and Economics* 10: 211–233.

Lord, C. G., L. Ross, and M. R. Lepper. 1979. "Biased Assimilation and Attitude Polarization: The Effects of Prior Theories on Subsequently Considered Evidence." *Journal of Personality and Social Psychology* 37: 2098–2109.

Lynch, Michael P. 2019. *Know-It-All Society.* New York: Liveright.

Mansbridge, Jane. 2010. "Deliberative Polling as the Gold Standard." *The Good Society* 19: 55–62.

Margalit, Avishai. 2010. *On Compromise and Rotten Compromises.* Princeton: Princeton University Press.

Margolis, Michele F. 2016. "Cognitive Dissonance, Elections, and Religion: How Partisanship and the Political Landscape Shape Religious Behaviors." *Public Opinion Quarterly* 80: 717–740.

Margolis, Michele F. 2018. *From Politics to the Pews.* Chicago: University of Chicago Press.

Marks, Joseph, Eloise Copland, Eleanor Loh, Cass Sunstein, and Tali Sharot. 2018. "Epistemic Spillovers: Learning Others' Political Views Reduces the Ability to Assess and Use Their Expertise in Nonpolitical Domains."

Harvard Public Law working paper. https://papers.ssrn.com/sol3/papers. cfm?abstract_id=3162009.

Marques, José M., Vincent Y. Yzerbyt, and Jacques-Philippe Leyens. 1988. "The 'Black Sheep Effect': Extremity of Judgments Towards Ingroup Members as a Function of Group Identification." *European Journal of Social Psychology* 18: 1–16.

Mason, Lilliana. 2015. "'I Disrespectfully Agree': The Differential Effects of Partisan Sorting on Social and Issue Polarization." *American Journal of Political Science* 59: 128–145.

Mason, Lilliana. 2018a. *Uncivil Agreement: How Politics Became Our Identity.* Chicago: University of Chicago Press.

Mason, Lilliana. 2018b. "Ideologues Without Issues: The Polarizing Consequences of Ideological Identities." *Public Opinion Quarterly* 82: 280–301.

Mason, Lilliana, and Julie Wronski. 2018. "One Tribe to Bind Them All: How Our Social Group Attachments Strengthen Partisanship." *Political Psychology* 39: 257–277.

McConnell, Christopher, Yotam Margalit, Neil Halhorta, and Matthew Levendusky. 2017. "The Economic Consequences of Partisanship in a Polarized Era." *American Journal of Political Science* 62: 5–18.

Mendelberg, Tali. 2002. "The Deliberative Citizen: Theory and Evidence." In *Research in Micropolitics*, vol. 6, *Political Decision Making, Deliberation, and Participation*. Edited by Michael X. Delli Carpini, Leonie Huddy, and Robert Y. Shapiro. Amsterdam: Elsevier.

Mill, John Stuart. (1859) 2015. *On Liberty and Other Essays.* New York: Oxford University Press.

Moscovici, S., and M. Zavalloni. 1969. "The Group as a Polarizer of Attitudes." *Journal of Personality and Social Psychology* 12: 125–135.

Mounk, Yascha. 2019. "Republicans Don't Understand Democrats—and Democrats Don't Understand Republicans." *The Atlantic*, June.

Mulligan, Thomas. 2018. "Plural Voting for the 21st Century." *Philosophical Quarterly* 68: 286–306.

Munro, Geoffrey D., Carrie Weih, and Jeffrey Tsai. 2010. "Motivated Suspicion: Asymmetrical Attributions of the Behavior of Political Ingroup and Outgroup Members." *Basic and Applied Social Psychology* 32: 173–184.

Mutz, Diana. 2006. *Hearing the Other Side: Deliberative Versus Participatory Democracy.* Cambridge, UK: Cambridge University Press.

Myers, D. G. 1975. "Discussion-Induced Attitude Polarization." *Human Relations* 28: 699–714.

Myers, D. G., and G. D. Bishop. 1970. "Discussion Effects on Racial Attitudes." *Science* 169.3947: 778–779.

Myers, D. G., J. B. Bruggink, R. C. Kersting, and B. A. Schlosser. 1980. "Does Learning Others' Opinions Change One's Opinion?" *Personality and Social Psychology Bulletin* 6: 253–260.

Neblo, Michael, Kevin M. Esterling, Ryan P. Kennedy, David M. J. Lazer, and Anana E. Sokhey. 2010. "Who Wants to Deliberate—and Why?" *American Political Science Review* 104: 566–583.

Nyhan, Brendan, and Jason Reifler. 2010. "When Corrections Fail: The Persistence of Political Misperceptions." *Political Behavior* 32: 303–330.

Orwell, George. (1946) 1968. "In Front of Your Nose." Reprinted in *In Front of Your Nose, vol. 4, 1945–1950*. Edited by Sonia Orwell and Ian Angus. Boston: Nonpareil Books.

Parkinson, John, and Jane Mansbridge, eds. 2012. *Deliberative Systems*. Cambridge, UK: Cambridge University Press.

Pettit, Philip. 2012. *On the People's Terms*. Cambridge, UK: Cambridge University Press.

Pew Research Center. 2014. "Political Polarization in the American Public." June 12. https://www.pewresearch.org/politics/2014/06/12/political-polarization-in-the-american-public/.

Pew Research Center. 2016. "Partisanship and Political Animosity in 2016." June 22. https://www.pewresearch.org/politics/2016/06/22/partisanship-and-political-animosity-in-2016/.

Pew Research Center. 2019a. "Partisan Antipathy: More Intense, More Personal." October 10. https://www.pewresearch.org/politics/2019/10/10/partisan-antipathy-more-intense-more-personal/.

Pew Research Center. 2019b. "Partisans Say Respect and Compromise Are Important in Politics—Particularly from Their Opponents." June 19. https://www.pewresearch.org/fact-tank/2019/06/19/partisans-say-respect-and-compromise-are-important-in-politics-particularly-from-their-opponents/.

Puglisi, Riccardo, and James M. Snyder. 2011. "Newspaper Coverage of Political Scandals." *Journal of Politics* 73: 931–950.

Rawls, John. 2005. *Political Liberalism*. Expanded ed. New York: Columbia University Press.

Schkade, David, Cass R. Sunstein, and Daniel Kahneman. 2000. "Deliberating About Dollars: The Severity Shift." *Columbia Law Review* 100: 1139–1175.

Sia, Choon-Ling, Bernard C. Y. Tan, and Kwok-Kee Wei. 2002. "Group Polarization and Computer-Mediated Communication: Effects of Communication: Cues, Social Presence, and Anonymity." *Information Systems Research* 13: 70–90.

Snedegar, Justin. 2018. "Reasons For and Reasons Against." *Philosophical Studies* 175: 725–743.

Sood, Guarav, and Shanto Iyengar. 2016. "Coming to Dislike Your Opponents: The Polarizing Impact of Political Campaigns." Unpublished working paper. https://www.gsood.com/research/papers/ComingToDislike.pdf.

Stanley, Matthew L., Peter S. Whitehead, Walter Sinnott-Armstrong, and Paul Seli. 2020. "Exposure to Opposing Reasons Reduces Negative

Impressions of Ideological Opponents." *Journal of Experimental of Psychology* 91: 104030.

Steiner, Jurg. 2012. *The Foundations of Deliberative Democracy*. Cambridge, UK: Cambridge University Press.

Sunstein, Cass R. 2009. *Going to Extremes: How Like Minds Unite and Divide*. New York: Oxford University Press.

Sunstein, Cass R. 2017. *#Republic*. Princeton: Princeton University Press.

Talisse, Robert B. 2019. *Sustaining Democracy: Why We Must Put Politics in Its Place*. New York: Oxford University Press.

Tam Cho, Wendy K., James G. Gimpel, and Iris S. Hui. 2013. "Voter Migration and the Geographic Sorting of the American Electorate." *Annals of the Association of American Geographers* 103: 856–870.

Tosi, Justin, and Brandon Warmke. 2020. *Grandstanding: The Use and Abuse of Moral Talk*. New York: Oxford University Press.

Turner, John C., Michael A. Hogg, Penelope J. Oakes, Stephen D. Reicher, and Margaret S. Wetherell. 1987. *Rediscovering the Social Group: A Self-Categorization Theory*. New York: Basil Blackwell.

Westfall, Jacob, Leaf Van Boven, John R. Chambers, and Charles M. Judd. 2015. "Perceiving Political Polarization in the United States: Party Identity Strength and Attitude Extremity Exacerbate the Perceived Partisan Divide." *Perspectives on Psychological Science* 10: 145–158.

Weston, Drew, Pavel S. Blagov, Keith Harenski, Clint Kilts, and Stephan Hamann. 2006. "The Neural Basis of Motivated Reasoning: An fMRI Study of Emotional Constraints on Political Judgment During the US Presidential Election of 2004." *Journal of Cognitive Neuroscience* 18: 1947–1958.

# Index